THE GREEN MOUNTAIN SPINNERY KNITTING BOOK

THE GREEN MOUNTAIN SPINNERY KNITTING BOOK

Contemporary and Classic Patterns

Margaret Klein Wilson and the Green Mountain Spinnery

THE COUNTRYMAN PRESS

WOODSTOCK, VERMONT

For Elizabeth Mills,
David Ritchie, Diana Wahle,
and Claire Wilson

Copyright © 2003 by Margaret Klein Wilson
and the Green Mountain Spinnery

First Edition

Library of Congress Cataloging-in-Publication Data:

Wilson, Margaret Klein.
   Green Mountain Spinnery knitting book : contem-
porary and classic patterns / Margaret Klein Wilson
   and the Green Mountain Spinnery. — 1st ed.
      p. cm.
   ISBN 0-88150-579-X
      1. Knitting—Patterns. 2. Sweaters. I. Green
   Mountain Spinnery. II. Title.
   TT825.W56 2003
   746.43'20432—dc21
                     2003046257

Cover design by Bren Frisch

Cover photo of Rebecca Rothfusz knitting Stained Glass
Sweater (Colorway 1) by Heidi Wells

Interior design by Eugenie S. Delaney

Art direction for all photography by Jillfrances Gray

Principal photography by Jeffrey Coolidge

Additional photography by Heidi Wells Photography, Inc.

Photograph on page x by Kindra Clineff

Schematics and chart graphics by Joy Wallens-Penford

Published by The Countryman Press, P.O. Box 748,
Woodstock, Vermont 05091

Distributed by W. W. Norton & Company,
500 Fifth Avenue, New York, NY 10110

Printed in Spain by Artes Graficas Toledo

10 9 8 7 6 5 4 3

CONTENTS

FOREWORD

Claire Wilson, David Ritchie, and Libby Mills, Green Mountain Spinnery founders and owners

The Green Mountain Spinnery is an anomaly in today's world, where lifestyles are shaped by high-speed travel, electronic communication, and disposable plastic goods. What is the reason for a business dedicated to the production of natural fiber yarns? What is our role?

Our Spinnery yarns are produced carefully, in small quantities, for craftspeople and artisans who work patiently with their hands. The goal of the Spinnery and of the knitters who use our product is to create functional, lastingly beautiful fabrics.

We find our work satisfying, even valuable. It has to do with our innate need for work rooted in the earth, in the natural cycles. The fibers for our yarns grow, literally, on sheep that flock and feed on pastures rich and poor. Seasonally, they are shorn of fleece as weather and breeding cycles decree; the wool arrives in its raw state, slippery with natural lanolin, with bits of hay and the lively scent of animals, all reminding us of our age-old dependence on agriculture and of our connection to the earth. We honor and celebrate that connection; it is the core of our existence.

Transforming the many types of raw fibers into luxurious and long-lasting yarn—that is the work and delight of the roughly one dozen people who are the Spinnery staff. The process is a specialized craft, collectively accomplished. Scourer, picker, carder, spinner, and finisher, each one contributes particular skills to the emerging product. Again, there is a connection, this time between people.

Then there is the relationship between the Spinnery and those who use the yarns. Within that community we have seen respect among individuals grow in mutual appreciation of each other's handwork. We have also seen inner horizons expanded, in awe of the handwork from countries and cultures foreign to our own.

Our Spinnery patterns draw on stitches, techniques, and skills from prehistoric times; the designs are inspired by age-old traditional garments. You as an artisan may widen your own horizons, stitch by stitch, as you turn our earth-based yarns into a fabric that, though personal, also reflects the continuity of craft. It is our hope that in knitting, weaving, felting, or simply resting your eyes on the glorious colors, you, the crafter, will sense this connection and be nourished.

As our hands follow the ancient rhythms of knitting and weaving we provide warmth, comfort, and beauty for our common humanity.

—Libby Mills with
David Ritchie and Claire Wilson
Green Mountain Spinnery

A Good Yarn

Stepping into the mill store of the Green Mountain Spinnery in Putney, Vermont, several things impress a visitor at once. There is the shop itself, a walk-in kaleidoscope of yarns, sweaters, and the tools of a knitter's practice: books, needles, patterns, and baskets bulging with the mill specials of the day. Then there is the peaty aroma of wool and lanolin, certain evidence of sheep and their life on the land. Lastly, there is the steady drone of spinning machinery just around the corner. Here, the Spinnery goes about its founding mission: to support two ancient but enduring traditions, agriculture and knitting.

Crossing the threshold from the shop into the production area, a visitor invariably needs a minute or two to take in the scene. There is brightly colored yarn everywhere, in a palette inspired by the landscape in four seasons, neatly moving through the final stages of production: steaming, drying, skeining, twisting, labeling, shipping. Then there is the bemused question: "You make the yarn right here?" The answer invites joining a conversation about farming and fibers that started more than twenty years ago and shows no signs of abating.

In 1975 Claire Wilson, a journeyman weaver, and Libby Mills, a longtime teacher and founder of the weaving program at The Putney School, were impressed by the yarns a friend had brought back from a small spinning mill in Sweden. Despite a resurgence in New England sheep farming, there was a distinct lack of local natural fiber yarn. Why couldn't they create such beautiful yarns in Vermont?

At the same time, David Ritchie and Diana Wahle, recent graduate students of the School for International Training in Brattleboro, were in a study group with Claire examining how individual choice of every kind relates to global issues. At the center of their discussion was E. F. Schumacher's *Small Is Beautiful: Economics as if People Mattered.* The text built a powerful case for revitalizing rural communities through the use of intermediate technology, and the creation of small, local industries. It spoke directly to their concerns about the shift in Vermont's economy away from agriculture.

The basics of Schumacher's "home" economics were elegantly simple: Identify and use regional, renewable resources; employ local people; design a workplace that could start up without vast amounts of capital; and reduce dependence on foreign oil. The nature of the work and workplace should encourage community self-reliance and environmental harmony.

By the late 1970s the Vermont sheep population was growing as small wool flocks replaced dairy herds. Here was a ready and renewable source of materials. "As we watched New England and Vermont show dramatic increases in sheep breeding, a local wool processing facility seemed the obvious next step," David recalls.

The 1976 fuel crisis was also a factor. "There was a gas shortage," remembers Libby, "yet most yarns were imported or petroleum-based." Making yarn from regional materials would conserve fuel in two ways: reduce the use of fuel to import yarns and replace yarns made of oil-based synthetics.

Opening a regional spinning mill fit neatly into the *Small Is Beautiful* criteria for intermediate technology. The four honed their vision of home economics: to produce and sell the finest American wool yarn from New England sheep, and to provide people with a choice of knitting and weaving yarns. By maintaining a small production scale, they would minimize adverse effects on the environment and the need for shipping raw materials over long distances. A spinning mill would support local agriculture in three ways: by providing a service not otherwise available in the area; by creating a market for regional fleece and fiber acquisition; and by encouraging diversified farming and cottage industries in similar ventures. Central to all of this was the creation of a vital workplace where workers could use and expand their skills.

For the next four years they gathered support for their idea and worked steadily through the process of opening what would become the nation's smallest woolen mill of that time. Talking with local shepherds, writing a business plan, and working with state and cooperative funding agencies encouraged them. More than twenty friends and neighbors offered financial support. "Everyone we talked with was behind our

idea," Diana says. "We never doubted we would succeed."

A significant challenge lay in identifying which machinery could create their ideal product: yarn that was lively, buoyant, and consistent in hand and texture without being overprocessed. Claire and Diana toured mills in Ireland and Wales, researching which equipment would spin yarn with a minimal amount of processing stress to the fibers and emphasize the fleece's natural qualities. In the face of rapidly changing textile technology, the availability of replacement parts for equipment was also a key consideration. "We concluded that the two-drum card would work for the type of fiber preparation we had in mind," Claire recalls.

The search for technical expertise also led them to Harrisville Yarns in nearby New Hampshire. Here they were generously offered the chance to gain experience and further refine their workplace vision in a practical way. Ray Phillips, a Harrisville employee and lifelong mill technician, offered to help them locate a spinnery's worth of equipment.

Claire fondly recalls summer evenings spent driving the back roads of New England with Ray, going from one textile mill to the next. Piece by piece, they accumulated a two-drum Davis and Furber 1916 carding machine, a 1951 Whiten Model E spinning frame, a water extractor, and early-1900s components for picking fiber, winding cones, and plying and skeining yarn.

After evaluating historic mill sites in the center of Putney, they purchased, ironically, an abandoned gas station next to

Ray Phillips at the carding machine

Interstate 91 to house the mill. Here the founders set about creating a spinnery. Ray supervised the placing of each machine in the mill's compact manufacturing space.

Six years of planning and market research finally came to fruition. On a snowy December day in 1981, the mill store opened for business. "The first year was wild," Claire remembers. "We had so much to learn about making yarn with these machines." Within a year Ray decided to work with the Spinnery full time to supervise and mentor the entire staff in the fine art of spinning yarn.

Touring the Spinnery today, a visitor will find the business fully engaged in meeting its founding goals, with vintage machinery producing well-crafted contemporary natural fiber blend yarns. All the fibers used —alpaca, wool, mohair, organic cotton, and Lyocel—are renewable and domestically grown. Every effort is made to purchase clean materials directly from individual growers. Encouraging new fiber producers is an ongoing priority. The 100 percent wool yarns are spun entirely from New England fleece. No chemicals are used to bleach, moth-proof, or shrink-proof yarns.

Fourteen staff, each with a specific talent for the technical aspects of spinning and a passion for fiber arts, work closely together to create what one customer calls "yarn that is real yarn." The fibers for each small "lot" or mill run are passed from hand to machine, person to process. At each stage of yarn production, there is attention, accommodation, and a nearly palpable affection for the character and sometimes quirky nature of the fibers and venerable machinery. Watching the precise transformation of raw materials into a skein of yarn is to understand how much every step matters.

Small is beautiful in the workplace, but the Spinnery's sense of the whole, as a bridge between agriculture and knitting, extends well beyond what is happening at the mill. Central to the founding vision is mentoring individual breeders in the design of custom yarns specific to their flocks and interests. Although many shepherds want to sell their raw fiber to the Spinnery outright, just as many want it returned to them as a product that will contribute to their farm's diversity and income. Over the years, the Spinnery has spun more than thirty different breeds of wool and other fibers for growers.

When the raw materials are precious, making a custom yarn has alchemy of its own. There is the challenge of perfectly matching fiber to machinery: staple length and fiber fineness to gearing ratios, spinning oil, stranding, and level of twist. Turning Churro, Shetland, Horned Dorset, Friesian, and Jacob fleece into distinctive yarns offers crafters some out-of-the-ordinary knitting choices and supports efforts to reestablish these rare breeds. For every lot of wool spun at the Spinnery, there is a shepherd with a farm and sheep grazing on fields, and often, a related cottage industry enlivening their local economy.

The highly specific needs of some clients have required trailblazing. Working with the Esprit clothing company in the mid-1990s to create an organically made product, Claire, Libby, and David developed a method of using a nonpetroleum oil for carding and spinning. This, plus removing petroleum from the scouring soap, resulted in the *GREENSPUN* process. Because of the Spinnery's groundbreaking efforts, the Northeast Organic Farming Association developed organic standards for yarn processing. Increasingly, sheep breeders now choose organic methods of animal husbandry and pasturing, understanding that the fiber they raise can also be spun organically.

Maintaining sound environmental practices through every step of production and supporting social causes are ongoing considerations at the Spinnery. All orders are shipped in recycled boxes from a local mailing company. Waste wool sent to a central Vermont mill is spun into the interior windings for baseballs. A more efficient water-saving scouring system was custom-built in 1991, followed by a lanolin-extracting wastewater system in 2001. Mill ends are directed to charitable organizations that teach knitting or donate knitted items. When a crisis erupted in Afghanistan in 2002, a special mill run was created for fund-raising to support relief efforts.

Maintaining an ongoing conversation with customers is also central to the day-to-day life of the Spinnery. The staff patiently field yarn and knitting questions seven days a week in the shop and on the phone. Every fall, the company hosts a knitters' weekend, three days of lively dialogue between knitters and a guest teacher. There is always something to talk about, some exchange that includes the customer in the process of spinning yarns and creating patterns.

"You make the yarn right here?" Yes. The answer to the question underlies the ancient but enduring connection of shepherds and agriculture to yarn makers and knitters. When their craft turns into artisanship, the result is more than functional. The yarn offers inspiration of its own, passing on its mantle of creativity to the next pair of hands.

Spinnery yarns inspire Spinnery patterns. The following designs are satisfying evidence that our friends and neighbors, local artists and designers, have taken knitting into their own hands. This pattern collection invites you to do the same.

"Knitting matters."

⌒

—KATHERINE COBEY

PATTERN DEVELOPMENT
From Our Hands to Your Hands

To celebrate the Spinnery's opening in 1981, Mrs. Idabelle Hegemann wrote and donated her "Toasty Socks" pattern. Her simple sock design set the tone for future patterns: classic but contemporary with a distinct Putney style. Idabelle also began the Spinnery's tradition of collaborating with friends and neighbors to create knitting patterns.

"We design patterns we need and want to wear," says Libby. To page through twenty years of Spinnery patterns is to revisit more than eighty inspired encounters between friends, neighbors, customers, and employees. Their practical and eclectic response to the lively texture and vivacious colors of the yarns has resulted in the Spinnery's most loved patterns.

The rich color palette of Mountain Mohair sparked Melissa Lumley's designs for the Stained Glass Pullover and her newest pattern, Green Mountain Gardens. "I love color. I am constantly looking to the natural world for color combinations or scouting out architectural shapes to inspire my pattern work."

Rosemary Ladd, Idabelle's granddaughter, needed an easy "big" sweater to dress up or down through long Putney winters. Her comfortable roll neck design, Rosemary's Middle-Sized Sweater, is a useful template for color and stitch experimenting.

Candace Brown's immediate need to outfit growing teenage daughters inspired her imaginative cardigan constructions in

two patterns: Moriah's Wildflower Sweater and Candace's Eyelet Sweater. A longtime employee, she credits the inspiration for her Welt Cap and the Punta Edged Hat designs to the bold color palettes found in Bolivian and Peruvian weaving.

Spinnery staff Maureen Clark and Eric Robinson were irresistibly drawn to the pleasant hand and bright colors of Cotton Comfort in designing Maureen's Socks and Eric's Glovelets.

Lisa Lloyd's fascination with how different materials affect the flex and depth of a cabled design inspired the Cable Weave Pullover and Putney Aran Tunic.

Libby and Claire have collaborated together on many patterns. Their design work is guided by the conviction that basic, classic shapes translated into clear, accurate patterns support every knitter's abilities. Libby credits the book *Knitting in the Old Way,* by Priscilla Gibson-Roberts, as an important influence in her own growth as a designer. "By documenting the evolution of the sweater, Roberts helped me understand the development of construction techniques, and put me on a course centered around the adaptation of traditional designs to Green Mountain Spinnery yarns."

Well written, accurate, and thoroughly tested, the patterns offer a range of knitting experiences for every level of knitter. At the same time, they encourage a friendly conversation between the knitter and the materials, leaving plenty of room for free-ranging digression and each knitter's creativity.

USING THE PATTERNS

Once you have pattern and yarn in hand, take some time to get acquainted with your materials. Read through the pattern. Check the size, using your favorite sweater as a guide to determine the correct measurements. Metric measurements are noted on the schematic drawings and in the pattern introductions, but not within the patterns themselves. Finished measurements and schematic numbers may differ. Finished measurements reflect a garment that has been assembled; schematics reflect the measurements of the pieces of the garments before they are assembled.

Familiarize yourself with any special techniques or stitches noted. Read the yarn label for fiber content and washing instructions. Save at least one of the labels for the dye lot name and number in case you need to buy more yarn. Wind a skein into a ball and knit a gauge swatch. If you just rolled your eyes at the words "gauge" and "swatch" and are thinking about skipping this step, please reconsider.

You are about to engage in a conversation between yourself, a thoughtfully written pattern, and a distinctive yarn of your choice. Working the gauge swatch is your opening gambit, the moment you take the knitting into your own hands. Once you achieve the correct gauge, you can proceed with confidence and cheerfully immerse yourself in knitting, reasonably sure the finished project will meet your expectations.

WORKING THE GAUGE SWATCH

Cast on enough stitches with the recommended needle size to make a swatch that is at least 4" (10 cm) square, or large enough to include several repeats of the pattern stitch *plus* 3–5 extra stitches to create a border on each edge. These extra stitches and several rows of Garter Stitch at the beginning and end of the swatch will give your swatch borders stability, making it easier to measure. If the project you are contemplating is to be knit on circular needles, work the swatch in the round.

When the swatch measures at least 4" (10 cm) square, bind off. Count the number of stitches in 4" in the swatch and write it down. Now wash the swatch in the same way that you plan to wash your sweater; many yarns "bloom" in soap and water, which can dramatically alter the size and shape of each stitch, thereby changing the gauge. It is this *final* gauge you are trying to achieve, not the prewashed gauge. Let the swatch dry, then smooth it flat without stretching.

Using a flat ruler, count the number of stitches across 4" (10 cm) in several places; divide this number by four, noting even a fraction of a stitch difference. (Half a stitch difference adds up: 4 sts per inch over 100 sts = 25 inches; 4½ sts per inch over 100 sts = 22.2 inches.) If you have fewer stitches per inch than recommended, reknit the swatch on smaller needles. If you have more stitches

per inch than recommended, reknit the swatch on larger needles. Take these differences in stride—many knitters routinely adjust up or down several needle sizes to achieve gauge. As you work through your project, periodically check the prewashed gauge of your fabric. If the piece measures larger or smaller than what the pattern indicates, take advantage of how forgiving knitting can be: Simply unravel as need be, make the necessary adjustments, and continue on again.

The goals of knitting are threefold: to enjoy your materials, to take pleasure in working with your hands in a peaceful, productive way, and to create a satisfying, well-crafted project. With that in mind, if your finished measurements are off by only the merest fraction of an inch or a stitch, don't worry. Relax, and forge ahead. As Claire's mother was fond of saying about minor knitting snafus, "It will never be noticed on a galloping horse."

Finally, save your swatch. Attach it to a piece of card stock, slip it into a clear page sleeve, and file it in a three-ring binder. Include the yarn label, a copy of your pattern notes, and commentary on the person or occasion that prompted your project. You'll build a journal of your creative work and a helpful portfolio of reference material. Eventually, you might consider knitting all your swatches together into a crazy quilt pillow or throw to create a fun, practical archive of your work.

Yarn Selections

The patterns in this book were designed for and inspired by specific Spinnery yarns. In several patterns, it is possible to use a variety of yarns. To duplicate the projects as they appear in these pages, work with the suggested yarns. Natural fibers are full of character: lustrous, elastic, soft, supple, and often bloomy. Because Spinnery yarns are made with minimal processing, the inherent liveliness of every fiber type is retained. When knit, each yarn fiber blend produces a distinct fabric.

Should you decide to use a different yarn, choose one that is similar in fiber content, weight, and suggested gauge. Work a test swatch of at least 4" (10 cm) with the recommended needle size to determine the suitability of your choice.

Caring for Handknits

Spinnery yarns are softer and more beautiful after being gently washed by hand. Garments knit with natural fiber yarns are easy to care for and wash. Gentle handwashing continues to soften the fibers and will greatly extend their life. Choose a mild or vegetable oil–based soap. Check your local yarn shop for specialty herb-scented and wool wash products that will provide natural moth-proofing. A mild dishwashing liquid without enzymes is also suitable.

Fill a deep sink, basin, or your washing machine with enough lukewarm water to cover the items to be washed. Using your washing machine as a sink, and the spin cycle to extract the water, shortens the washing and drying time. Add a small amount of soap and agitate the water to make a sudsy bath. If you are using your washing machine, *turn off the machine now.* Immerse the garment, gently submerging and squeezing the water through until it is completely saturated. Soak for 10–20 minutes. Drain the water from the sink, or spin out the water from your washing machine using the gentle cycle in short bursts as needed. Repeat this process without soap to rinse. Gather up your washed item in a towel and transfer to a drying screen or lay it on heavy towels on a flat surface in a well-ventilated area. Carefully shape to measurements. When the garment is nearly dry you may decide to turn it inside out to complete the drying process.

Storing Woolens

Wash and completely dry your woolens before storing them for any length of time. Fold the items flat and then store in a container that allows the materials to breathe. A cedar chest is the perfect storage space but if that is not available, tuck the sweater in a zippered cloth bag with a cedar block. Sand the block lightly if the scent has faded. A mixture of aromatic herbs such as lavender and pennyroyal wrapped in muslin is a known moth deterrent. Storing wool in closed but not tightly sealed cardboard boxes with herbal sachets and topped with a sheet of brown craft paper is also a good, short-term storage option. The fibers can breathe, and it is our experience that moths have no appetite for cardboard. Check your garments periodically to look for evidence of moths and to freshen sachets.

Knitting Techniques

The following basic techniques and standard finishing methods are featured in many Spinnery patterns.

Kitchener Stitch

This method of joining makes a knit row that blends two pieces together with an almost invisible seam. Using this method to finish socks will create a smooth, comfortable toe.

Hold your needles parallel to each other with points in the same direction, and yarn at the right end of back needle. Using a tapestry needle, weave together the two pieces as follows:

Set Up: Pass the yarn through the first stitch on the front needle purlwise and then through the first stitch of the back needle knitwise. Pull yarn through, but do not pull it tight.

1. Pass the yarn through the first st of front needle a second time, knitwise, and then slip st off needle.
2. Pass the yarn through the second st on front needle purlwise; leave st on needle and pull yarn through.
3. Pass the yarn through the first st on back needle a second time purlwise; slip st off needle.
4. Pass the yarn through second st of back needle knitwise; leave st on needle. Pull the yarn firm.

Repeat steps 1–4 until no more stitches remain. When you have completed the graft, go back and smooth the stitches to make them match your knitting gauge. With proper tension on the yarn, these woven stitches will look just like your knitted stitches.

Steeks

For centuries, traditional knitters from many cultures have used steeks as a method of knitting in the round easily with many colors in a charted design. Steeks create seam allowances at the armholes, neck, and cardigan openings that are later cut open and stitched down: A cardigan or pullover can be knit in a tube. You have the pleasure of looking at the right side of your work as you watch the charted designs grow in your hands. With the pattern in front at all times, it is easy to check the accuracy of your knitting. Working in the round also helps the knitter achieve a more consistent row gauge. If you've never worked steeks before, experiment on a swatch. This technique is truly safe and easy!

Making a steek: Bind off the recommended number of stitches at the armhole and neck openings. On the next round, cast on the same number of stitches over the bound off stitches, placing markers on either side of these stitches. Every time you come to the marker, work the first stitch in the background color of the row you are currently working, then work the middle stitches by alternating the colors of that row, and end with the background color. When the knitting is finished, hand-sew or machine-stitch a row of stitches the length of the steek on both sides of the center steek stitch. Cut the steek between these two lines. Have no fear: Natural fibers hold together and will not unravel. Fold the cut edges back. To work

sleeves and neckbands, pick up stitches between the garment stitches and the first/last steek stitches. When you have finished knitting the sleeves and neckbands, trim the steeks. Roll the edges back and baste down evenly using a tapestry needle.

Three Needle Bind Off

This standard technique for joining shoulders creates a tidy seam by knitting two sets of an equal number of stitches together, usually working with the right sides of the material together. Using two straight needles of any size, place stitches for one back shoulder on one needle and stitches for the corresponding front shoulder on the second needle, with needles pointing to the right. Hold these two needles together. With a third needle, knit into the first stitch on the front needle and the first stitch on the back needle. Knit these two stitches together. Repeat and pass the first stitch over the second stitch. Continue to bind off in this manner until one stitch remains. Cut the yarn and pull it through the last stitch.

Two variations on this method create a different look to the finished bound off shoulder. Purling the stitches while working the bind off makes a flatter seam. Holding the wrong sides of the work together while binding off creates a decorative ridge.

Increases and Decreases

m1: Make one.

m1 right: Insert the left needle from back to front under the bar between the st just worked and the next st and knit this strand through the front.

m1 left: Insert the left needle from front to back under the bar between the st just worked and the next st and knit this strand through the back.

ssk: Slip 2 sts, one at a time, as if to knit; insert left needle into front of sts and knit together (left-slanted decrease).

ssp: Slip 2 sts, one at a time, as if to purl; insert left needle into front of sts and purl together.

yo: yarn over. On right side, bring yarn to front between needles before knitting next stitch; take yarn to the back by placing it over the right needle; then work the next stitch.

Abbreviations

C	circular needle	mm	millimeters	tbl	through back loop
CC	contrasting color	NB	nota bene (take note)	WS	wrong side
ch	crochet hook	oz	ounce(s)	wyib	with yarn in back
cm	centimeter	p	purl	wyif	with yarn in front
cn	cable needle	PS	Pattern Stitch	XL	X-Large
DC	darker color	p2tog	Purl two stitches together	yds	yards
dec	decrease(s), decreasing	patt	pattern	yo	yarn over
DK	double-knitting weight	pm	place marker(s)		
dpn	double pointed needle(s)	psso	pass slipped st over		
epi	ends per inch	rem	remaining		
inc	increase(s), increasing	reps	repeats		
k	knit	rev	reverse		
k2tog	knit 2 sts together (right-slanted decrease)	rh	right hand		
		RS	right side		
LC	lighter color	S	straight needle		
Lg	Large	sc	single crochet		
lh	left hand	sett	warp ends per inch		
MC	main color	sl	slip		
Med	Medium	Sm	small		
m1	make one	sp	spare		
m1 right:	Insert the left needle from back to front under the bar between the st just worked and the next st and purl this strand through the front.	ssk	Slip 2 sts, one at a time, as if to knit; insert left needle into front of sts and knit tog (left-slanted decrease).		
m1 left:	Insert the left needle from front to back under the bar between the st just worked and the next st and purl this strand through the back.	ssp	Slip 2 sts, one at a time, as if to purl; insert left needle into front of sts and purl tog.		
		St st	Stockinette Stitch		
		st(s)	stitch(es)		
		tog	together		

The Patterns

Artisan's Vest, Spinnery
Jacket & Cozy Vest

ARTISAN'S VEST

(Pictured in Moonshadow Sylvan Spirit)

A vertical Seed Stitch pattern gives this classic unisex pattern interest without complexity: Pick it up, knit it anywhere, and finish it quickly. Short row shaping at the shoulders ensures perfect drape and a comfortable fit in several types of yarn.

An easy pattern.

FINISHED MEASUREMENTS

Chest: 36 (40, 44, 48, 52)"/91.5 (101.5, 112, 122, 132) cm

Length to shoulder: 19½ (20½, 22, 24½, 25½)"/49.5 (52, 56, 62, 64) cm

GAUGE

20 sts & 28 rows = 4" (10 cm) in St st

MATERIALS

Yarn

Cotton Comfort or Sylvan Spirit: 3 (4, 5, 5, 6) 2 oz skeins

Mountain Mohair: 4 (6, 7, 7, 8) 2 oz skeins

Double Twist or 2-Ply Wool: 2 (3, 4, 4, 5) 4 oz skeins

Green Mountain Green: 4 (6, 8, 8, 9) 2 oz skeins

Needles: Sizes 5 (3.75 mm) & 6 (4.0 mm) 29" (80 cm) circular, or sizes needed to obtain gauge

Crochet hook: Size E

Stitch holders: 3 large

Buttons: 5 (5, 5, 6, 6) ⅝"/1.3 cm

CAST ON 180 (200, 220, 240, 260) sts, using Size 5 needle. Work Seed Stitch as follows:

Row 1: *K1, p1, repeat from *.
Row 2: *P1, k1, repeat from *.

Alternate these 2 rows for 1 inch. Then change to Size 6 needle and work in Rib Pattern as follows:

RIB PATTERN

Row 1: K2, p1, *k4, p1, repeat from * 35 (39, 43, 47, 51) times, knit last 2 sts.
Row 2: Purl all sts.

Alternate these 2 rows until entire piece

Artisan's Vest, Spinnery Jacket & Cozy Vest— *Elizabeth Mills and Claire Wilson, Spinnery co-owners, have designed and written more than thirty patterns together since the company's founding in 1981. Here, their trio of jacket and vests is an elegant demonstration of what a simple design partnered with the right yarn can achieve.*

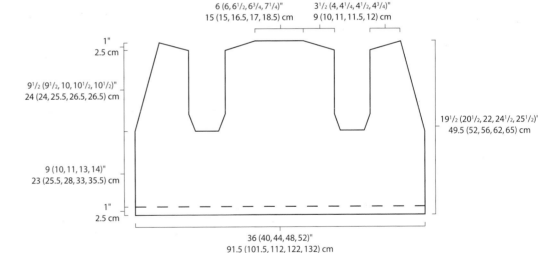

6 (6, 6½, 6¾, 7¼)"
15 (15, 16.5, 17, 18.5) cm

3½ (4, 4¼, 4½, 4¾)"
9 (10, 11, 11.5, 12) cm

1"
2.5 cm

9½ (9½, 10, 10½, 10½)"
24 (24, 25.5, 26.5, 26.5) cm

19½ (20½, 22, 24½, 25½)"
49.5 (52, 56, 62, 65) cm

9 (10, 11, 13, 14)"
23 (25.5, 28, 33, 35.5) cm

1"
2.5 cm

36 (40, 44, 48, 52)"
91.5 (101.5, 112, 122, 132) cm

measures 10 (11, 12, 14, 15) inches, or 9 (9½, 10, 10½, 10½) inches less than desired length to shoulder, ending with Row 2.

DIVIDE FOR FRONT AND BACK

Keeping in Rib Pattern, work across 38 (43, 47, 51, 56) sts and place these sts on holder for Right Front. Bind off the following 14 (14, 16, 18, 18) sts. Work across 90 (100, 110, 120, 130) sts for Back; place rem 38 (43, 47, 51, 56) sts on holder for Left Front.

BACK

Bind off 14 (14, 16, 18, 18) sts; work to end of row. There are 76 (86, 94, 102, 112) sts. On the following row, dec as follows: k1, ssk, work to the last 3 sts, k2tog, k1. Repeat this dec every other row until 66 (70, 74, 80, 84) sts remain. Continue in Rib Pattern until armhole measures 9½ (9½, 10, 10½, 10½) inches, ending with a purl row.

Shape shoulders by working short rows as follows: Work across 60 (64, 67, 73, 76) sts; turn, sl the first st, and purl back across 53 (57, 59, 65, 68) sts; turn, sl the first st, and work Rib across 47 (50, 52, 58, 60) sts; turn, sl the first st, and purl across 41 (43, 45, 51, 52) sts; turn, sl the first st, and work Rib across 35 (36, 38, 42, 44) sts; turn, sl 1, work 29 (29, 31, 32, 36) sts; turn, sl 1, work to end of row, 47 (49, 52, 57, 61) sts. Place sts on a holder.

LEFT FRONT

Transfer sts from holder to needle and begin dec at armhole edge: Knit 1, ssk, work to end of row. Continue dec at armhole every other row 5 (8, 10, 11, 14) times. *At the same time,* dec at neck edge every fourth row by working to within 3 sts of end of row, k2tog, k1. Continue dec at neck edge until 18 (20, 21, 23, 24) sts remain. Continue straight until armhole measures 9½ (9½, 10, 10½, 10½) inches. Place sts on holder.

RIGHT FRONT

Transfer sts from holder to needle and, beginning on a WS row, work to correspond to Left Front. Work dec on RS rows. Decrease for neck edge by beginning the row k1, ssk. Decrease for armhole by knitting to within 3 sts of end of row, k2tog, k1.

JOIN SHOULDERS

With RS together, join shoulders using the Three Needle Bind Off. When first shoulder is knit together, bind off the next 30 (30, 32, 34, 36) sts for Back neck. Knit pieces of the second shoulder together as you did the first.

FINISHING

Using Size E ch and working firmly, sc up the Front edge, around neck, and down second Front edge. Work a second row of sc, making 5 (5, 5, 6, 6) evenly spaced buttonholes on Right Front for women's vest and Left Front for men's. Form the buttonholes by crocheting a chain of 4 sts to form a loop. Attach the loop to the edge of the garment by crocheting through the edge. Continue to the next buttonhole repeat. Work 2 rows of sc around armholes. Weave in loose ends. Sew on buttons.

For washing instructions read "Caring for Handknits" on page xiv.

SPINNERY JACKET

(Pictured in Blizzard Mountain Mohair on page 2)

Formal or fun, this basic cardigan features vertical lines of Seed Stitch, picked up sleeves, and short row shaping in the shoulders. A knit "polo" collar and crocheted front bands finish the jacket. Worked up in sturdy Yarn Over or bloomy, colorful Mountain Mohair, this is the sweater you will always be happy to have close at hand.

An easy pattern.

FINISHED MEASUREMENTS
Chest: 34 (38, 42, 46, 50, 54)"/86.5 (96.5, 106.5, 117, 127, 137) cm

Length to underarm: 13 (14, 15, 16, 16½, 18)"/33 (35.5, 38, 40.5, 42, 45.5) cm

Length to shoulder: 22 (24, 26, 27, 28, 30)"/56 (61, 66, 68.5, 71, 76) cm

GAUGE
16 sts & 20 rows = 4" (10 cm) in St st

MATERIALS
Yarn

Mountain Mohair: 8 (9, 11, 11, 12, 13) 2 oz skeins

Yarn Over: 7 (7, 8, 8, 9, 10) 4 oz skeins

Needles: Sizes 6 (4 mm) & 7 (4.5 mm) straight, or sizes needed to obtain gauge; 1 spare straight needle any size

Crochet hook: Size G

Stitch holders: 2 small, 1 large

Buttons: 6 (6, 7, 7, 7, 8) ¾"/1.9 cm

BACK
CAST ON 71 (79, 86, 94, 103, 111) sts using larger needle. Begin with a WS row, and work in patt as follows until piece measures 13 (14, 15, 16, 16½, 18) inches, or desired length to underarm.

Pattern Stitch
WS rows: Purl.

RS rows: K5 (4, 5, 4, 6, 5), p1, *k4, p1, repeat from * 12 (14, 15, 17, 18, 20) times, k5 (4, 5, 4, 6, 5).

Armhole: Bind off 8 (7, 8, 10, 12, 12) sts at beginning of the next 2 rows. There are 55 (65, 70, 74, 79, 87) sts. Work straight until armhole measures 8 (9½, 10½, 10½, 11, 11½) inches, ending with a purl (WS) row.

Shape shoulder: Work short rows as follows:
Row 1: Work to within 8 (10, 11, 11, 12, 13) sts of end of row. Wrap the next st by

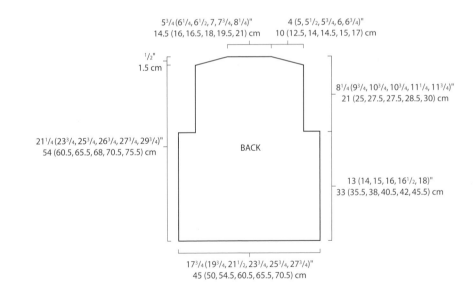

slipping it as if to purl, bringing the yarn forward and laying it over knitted piece, then moving the slipped st back to left needle. Turn work.

Row 2: Purl to within 8 (10, 11, 11, 12, 13) sts of end of row. Wrap the next st by slip-

ping the st as if to purl, taking the yarn to back of work, then moving the slipped st back to left needle. Turn work.

Row 3: Work to within 16 (20, 22, 23, 24, 27) sts of end of row; wrap st as in Row 1. Turn work.

Row 4: Purl to within 16 (20, 22, 23, 24, 27) sts of end of row; wrap st as in Row 2. Turn work.

Row 5: This row hides the wraps on the RS row. Work to the wrapped st. Insert needle under the wrap and knit it together with the st. Work in this way to end of row.

Row 6: This row hides the wraps on the WS row. Purl to the wrapped st. Insert the needle from behind, into the back loop of the wrap, and place it on the left needle. Purl the wrap and the st together. Work in this way to end of row.

Place all 55 (65, 70, 74, 79, 87) sts on large holder. There are 16 (20, 22, 23, 24, 27) sts for each shoulder.

RIGHT FRONT
PATTERN STITCH

WS rows: Purl.
RS rows: K5 (5, 3, 3, 5, 5), p1, *k4, p1, repeat from * 5 (6, 7, 8, 8, 9) times, end row k5 (4, 5, 4, 6, 5).

CAST ON 36 (40, 44, 48, 52, 56) sts. Begin with a WS row, and work in patt until piece measures same as Back to underarm, ending with a RS row. On the following row, bind off 8 (7, 8, 10, 12, 12) sts. There are 28 (33, 36, 38, 40, 44) sts. Work straight on rem sts until armhole measures 5 (6, 6½, 6½, 7, 7) inches, ending with a WS row.

Shape Neck
Bind off 5 (6, 7, 7, 8, 9) sts. Then dec on the following 7 (7, 7, 8, 8, 8) RS rows at neck edge as follows: k2, ssk, knit to end of row.

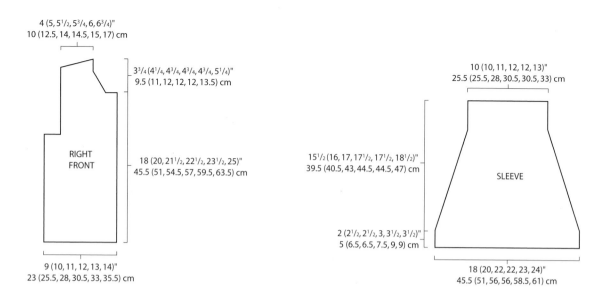

4 (5, 5½, 5¾, 6, 6¾)"
10 (12.5, 14, 14.5, 15, 17) cm

3¾ (4¼, 4¾, 4¾, 4¾, 5¼)"
9.5 (11, 12, 12, 12, 13.5) cm

RIGHT FRONT

18 (20, 21½, 22½, 23½, 25)"
45.5 (51, 54.5, 57, 59.5, 63.5) cm

9 (10, 11, 12, 13, 14)"
23 (25.5, 28, 30.5, 33, 35.5) cm

10 (10, 11, 12, 12, 13)"
25.5 (25.5, 28, 30.5, 30.5, 33) cm

15½ (16, 17, 17½, 17½, 18½)"
39.5 (40.5, 43, 44.5, 44.5, 47) cm

SLEEVE

2 (2½, 2½, 3, 3½, 3½)"
5 (6.5, 6.5, 7.5, 9, 9) cm

18 (20, 22, 22, 23, 24)"
45.5 (51, 56, 56, 58.5, 61) cm

There are 16 (20, 22, 23, 24, 27) sts. Work straight until armhole measures same as Back, ending with a purl row.

NB: The shoulder-shaping process results in one more row on left shoulder than on right.

Shape Shoulder
Work short rows as follows:
Row 1: Same as Row 1 for shaping shoulders for Back.
Row 2: Purl all sts.
Row 3: Same as Row 5 for Back.
Place sts on holder.

LEFT FRONT
CAST ON as for Right Front and work to correspond. RS rows of pattern will be: k5 (4, 5, 4, 6, 5), p1, *k4, p1, repeat from * 5 (6, 7, 8, 8, 9) times, ending row k5 (5, 3, 3, 5, 5) sts.

Binding off for armhole will be on RS row. Binding off for neck will be on WS row.

Decrease at neck edge on RS rows as follows: Knit to within 4 sts of end of row, k2tog, k2.

Shape Shoulder
Row 1: Working on a WS row, purl to within 8 (10, 11, 11, 12, 13) sts of end of row. Wrap the next st by slipping the st as if to purl, taking the yarn to back of work, then moving the slipped st back to left needle. Turn work.
Row 2: Knit all sts.
Row 3: Work same as Row 6 for shaping shoulders for Back.

Join Shoulders
With RS together, join shoulders using the Three Needle Bind Off method. When first shoulder is joined, bind off 23 (25, 26, 28, 31, 33) sts for Back neck. Then knit and

bind off sts for second shoulder. Break yarn and pull end through last st.

SLEEVE

With larger (Size 7) needles and RS of work facing you, pick up and k72 (80, 88, 88, 92, 96) sts along the straight edge of armhole. Do not pick up the bound off sts at underarm. Work in patt for 2 (2½, 2½, 3, 3½, 3½) inches, ending with a WS row. The next row is a dec row. Work as follows: Knit 1, sl 1, k1, psso, work to within 3 sts of end of row, k2tog, k1.

Work a dec row every 6 (6, 4, 4, 4, 4) rows 16 (20, 22, 20, 22, 22) times. There are 40 (40, 44, 48, 48, 52) sts. Work straight until sleeve measures 17½ (18½, 19½, 20½, 21, 22) inches, or desired length, ending with a RS row. Bind off while knitting all sts.

COLLAR

With RS of work facing and using larger (Size 7) needle, pick up and k5 (6, 7, 7, 8, 9) bound off sts at Front neck edge; pick up and k18 (19, 21, 21, 23, 23) sts to shoulder seam; pick up and k23 (25, 26, 28, 31, 33) bound off sts for Back neck; pick up and k18 (19, 20, 22, 23, 23) sts from shoulder seam to bound off sts at Front neck edge; pick up and k5 (6, 7, 7, 8, 9) bound off sts at Front neck edge. There are 69 (75, 81, 85, 93, 97) sts. Purl 1 row. Change to smaller needle. Work 3 rows of p1, k1 rib. (The first row will begin and end with a purl st; the second row will begin and end with a

knit st.) Change to larger needles and begin inc at each end of Collar as follows: k1, p1, k1, m1 st, work to within 3 sts of end of row, m1 st, k1, p1, k1. Increase in this way a total of 6 times, keeping the 3 sts at each end of Collar k1, p1, k1 on RS rows, and p1, k1, p1 on WS rows. Work the inc sts into the rem Rib Pattern. There are 81 (87, 93, 97, 105, 109) sts. Work straight for 7 rows. Bind off in ribbing.

FINISHING

Join sleeve and side seams. Beginning at underarm, the first 2 (2, 2, 2½, 3, 3) inches of sleeve will be joined to the bound off sts for armhole. If desired, the side seams may be left open for 3 or 4 inches from the bottom edge, and the open edges worked with single crochet.

With RS of work facing, make 2 rows of sc in Yarn Over or 3 rows in Mountain Mohair along Front edges. Work from edge of Collar to bottom edge of jacket on Left Front. Work from bottom edge to Collar on Right Front. Work 6 (6, 7, 7, 7, 8) buttonholes, evenly spaced, in the second row of sc on Right Front for woman's jacket, on Left Front for man's jacket. Place the bottom buttonhole 3½ (3½, 3½, 4, 4½, 4½) inches from bottom edge of jacket. Weave in loose ends. Sew on buttons.

For washing instructions read "Caring for Handknits" on page xiv.

COZY VEST

(Pictured in Poppy Double Twist Wool on page 2)

The double thick, cuddly fabric of this unisex vest comes from a simple Slip Stitch ribbing pattern offered by Barbara G. Walker in *A Second Treasury of Knitting Patterns*. Two design elements—slits at the hip and optional side gussets—offer three shaping alternatives for various body types. Knitters may knit the vest straight up and down, create side gussets to accommodate a larger chest measurement, or leave panels open to waistline to allow for larger hip size.

An easy pattern.

SIZES
Small (Medium, Large, X-Large)

FINISHED MEASUREMENTS
Without gusset: 35 (39½, 44, 49)"/89 (100.5, 112, 124.5) cm
Length to underarm: 11 (12, 13, 14)"/28 (30.5, 33, 35.5) cm
Length to shoulder: Approx 20 (21½, 23, 24½)"/51 (54.5, 58.5, 62) cm
With gusset: Each inc row for the gusset will add an inch to the chest measurement. Add as many inc as needed.

GAUGE
26 sts & 26 rows = 4" (10 cm) in PS

MATERIALS
Yarn
Double Twist or 2-Ply Wool: 5 (6, 7, 8) 4 oz skeins
Mountain Mohair: 10 (11, 12, 14) 2 oz skeins
Green Mountain Green: 11 (13, 14, 16) 2 oz skeins
Needles: Size 7 (4.5 mm) circular, 29" or 36", or sizes needed to obtain gauge; 3 spare needles of any size
Stitch holders: 2 small, 4 large
Buttons: 5 or 6 large, 9 or 10 small, ½" to 1" (1.5 cm to 2.5 cm)

PATTERN STITCH (PS) WITH ODD NUMBER OF STS
Row 1 (RS): K1, *sl 1 as if to purl, wyib, k1; rep from *.
Row 2 (WS): K1, *p1, k1; rep from *.
Three panels—two for the front and a longer one for the back—are worked separately, then joined and worked together in the body of the vest.

PANELS
Back: CAST ON 111 (127, 143, 159) sts. Work in PS for 4 inches (6 inches if deeper panels are desired), ending with Row 2. Put all sts on a spare needle.

Left Front: CAST ON 57 (65, 73, 81) sts. Work in PS for 2 inches (4 inches if deeper panels are desired), ending with Row 2. Put these sts on second spare needle.

Right Front: Make a second piece the same as Left Front.

JOIN PANELS
Without gusset: Work Row 1 of PS across Right Front, pm on needle; continue in PS across back, pm on needle, continue in PS across Left Front. There are 225 (257, 289, 321) sts, with 2 knit sts (now they look like purl sts) between Back and Fronts. Work Row 2 of PS.

Next row, create seam st: Work across Right Front to marker, m1 st. Work across Back to marker, m1 st. Work across Left Front. On next row, purl these two new "made" sts; they are the underarm "seam" sts. Continue working Body, slipping the new seam sts on Row 1, purling them on Row 2.

With optional shaped gusset: Work in PS for 1 inch, or until work measures 1 inch above waistline, ending with Row 2.

Increase each side of seam st as follows: Work 56, (64, 72, 80) sts of Right Front, pm on needle, m1, work 3 sts of gusset in patt, m1, pm on needle, work 109 (125, 141, 157) back sts, pm on needle, m1, work 3 sts of gusset in patt, m1, pm, and work to end of row. On Row 2, knit the new "made" sts. These will be knit sts on Row 1 also. Continue inc in this manner every 1½

8

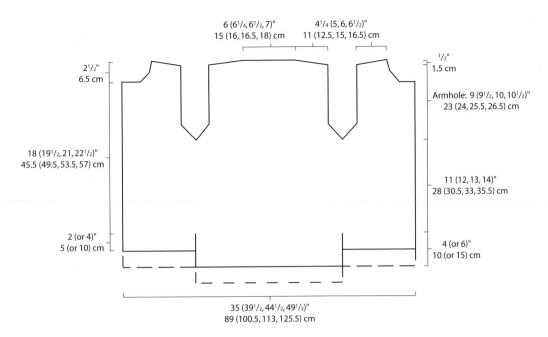

Diagram measurements:

- 6 (6¼, 6½, 7)" 15 (16, 16.5, 18) cm
- 4¼ (5, 6, 6½)" 11 (12.5, 15, 16.5) cm
- 2½" 6.5 cm
- ½" 1.5 cm
- Armhole: 9 (9½, 10, 10½)" 23 (24, 25.5, 26.5) cm
- 18 (19½, 21, 22½)" 45.5 (49.5, 53.5, 57) cm
- 11 (12, 13, 14)" 28 (30.5, 33, 35.5) cm
- 2 (or 4)" 5 (or 10) cm
- 4 (or 6)" 10 (or 15) cm
- 35 (39½, 44½, 49½)" 89 (100.5, 113, 125.5) cm

inches, always adding sts at the outside edge of gussets. This will give a clean line to a Garter Stitch gusset. Continue to sl the seam st on Row 1 and purl it on Row 2.

DIVIDE FOR FRONT AND BACK

When work measures 11 (12, 13, 14) inches from the joining of panels, or desired length to armhole, and ending with Row 2 of PS, divide for Front and Back.

With gusset: Beginning on Row 1, work across 57 (65, 73, 81) Right Front sts to gusset, ending k1, and place these sts on a large holder. Bind off all but the last st of gusset, k2tog tbl; work across rem 110 (126, 142, 158) Back sts to gusset, ending k1. Place rem sts on a large holder.

Without gusset: Work across Right Front, place these sts on a holder, bind off the seam st by knitting it, knit the following st, pass seam st over. Work across rem 110 (126, 142, 158) sts for back and place rem sts on a holder for Left Front.

BACK YOKE

Work Row 2 of PS. Then begin to shape armholes, using Decrease A at beginning of row, Decrease B at end of row.

Decrease A (used at RS of work, RS facing)
Row 1: K1, sl 1, k2tog tbl, resume PS.
Row 2: Work in PS to last 3 sts of row, p2, k1.
Row 3: K1, sl 1, k2tog tbl, sl 1, resume PS.
Row 4: Same as Row 2 of PS.

Decrease B is used at left side of work, RS facing:
Rows 1 & 3: Work in PS to last 4 sts, k2tog, sl 1, k1.
Row 2: K1, p2, resume PS.

Row 4: Same as Row 2 of PS.
Work 8 (10, 12, 14) dec, leaving 95 (107, 119, 131) sts on needle. Continue in PS until armhole measures 9 (9½ 10, 10½) inches or desired length, ending with Row 2.

Shape shoulders by working short rows as follows:
Row 1 (RS): Work in PS to last 10 (12, 14, 16) sts. Wrap the next st by slipping it as if to purl, bringing the yarn forward and laying it over knitted piece, then returning st to left needle. Turn work.
Row 2 (WS): Work in PS to last 10 (12, 14, 16) sts. Wrap next st as in Row 1; turn work.
Row 3: Work in PS to last 20 (24, 28, 32) sts. Wrap next st as in Row 1; turn work.
Row 4: Work in PS to last 20 (24, 28, 32) sts. Wrap next st as in Row 1; turn work.
Row 5: Work in PS to last 28 (33, 38, 43) sts. Wrap next st as in Row 1; turn work.
Row 6: Work in PS to last 28 (33, 38, 43) sts. Put rem sts on a holder for right shoulder. Put 39 (41, 43, 45) center sts on a holder for neck. Put rem 28 (33, 38, 43) sts on a holder for left shoulder.

LEFT FRONT YOKE

With gusset: Attach yarn and bind off all but the last st of gusset; knit this last st together with next st tbl; work in PS to end of row. There are 57 (65, 73, 81) sts.

Without gusset: Attach yarn, bind off the seam st by knitting it, knitting the next st, and passing the seam st over. Complete the row in PS. There are 57 (65, 73, 81) sts.

With and without gusset: Work Row 2 of PS. On the following row, begin Decrease A. Continue dec for a total of 8 (10, 12, 14) times. There are 49 (55, 61, 67) sts. Work until armhole measures 7 (7½, 8, 8½) inches, ending Row 1. Next row, work across first 12 (12, 12, 14) sts, place them on a small holder, and complete row. On the following row, begin Decrease B and continue for a total of 9 (10, 11, 10) dec. There are 28 (33, 38, 43) sts. At the same time, begin shoulder shaping when armhole measures 9 (9½, 10, 10½) inches.

Row 1 (WS): Work to last 10 (12, 14, 16) sts, wrap st, turn.

Row 2: Work in PS to end of row.

Row 3: Work to last 20 (24, 28, 32) sts, wrap st, turn.

Row 4: Work in PS to end of row.

Put all sts on spare needle.

RIGHT FRONT YOKE

Attaching new ball of yarn and beginning at armhole edge with WS facing, work Row 2 of PS. Then shape Right Front as a mirror image of Left Front, using Decrease B at armholes, Decrease A at neckline. Rows 1 and 3 of shoulder shaping will be worked on RS rows.

JOIN SHOULDERS

Using spare needles, place sts for Back on one and Fronts on the other, with WS together. The seam st or ridge created by joining the shoulders using the Three Needle Bind Off method will be on the outside, and is a design element. Knit together loosely the first st from front and back needles, then *loosely k4tog, 2 sts from each needle, pass first st over second; repeat from *. Bind off in this manner until all sts for one shoulder are bound off. Repeat for second shoulder.

COLLAR

Beginning at Right Front neck edge, with RS facing, transfer the 12 (12, 12, 14) sts from small holder to needle; attach yarn, then pick up and k15 sts from Front neck, including shoulder seam; work the sts for Back neck in patt; pick up and k15 sts along left neck edge; work the 12 (12, 12, 14) sts for Left Front neck from small holder in patt. Work next row as Row 2 of pattern. (If necessary, add or drop a picked up st along either neck edge to keep the sts in patt.) Continue in patt for 2½ inches, or until Collar reaches desired height, ending Row 2. Bind off as follows: With RS facing, k1 loosely, *k2tog tbl loosely, pass first st over, repeat from * to end of row.

FINISHING

Weave loose ends into fabric. Leaving gusset sts as is, work 1 row sc along armhole sides. Mark places for buttons evenly spaced between bottom of Collar and bottom of vest. Work 2 rows sc along each Front edge, making each buttonhole by replacing a sc with enough chain sts to accommodate your button choice.

For washing instructions read "Caring for Handknits" on page xiv.

Easy Raglan & Stained Glass—Elizabeth Mills introduces contemporary touches to a classic "top down" raglan pattern, creating a unisex pullover that lives up to its name for all ages and sizes. Melissa Lumley's pattern combines a pleasing color palette with an age-old knitting technique that makes multi-color knitting simple.

*Easy Raglan
& Stained Glass
Pullover*

EASY RAGLAN

(Child model pictured in Blue Violet Mountain Mohair; Adult model pictured in Blue Gentian Mountain Mohair)

Knit from the top down in one piece, this basic raglan for adults and children features two choices for neck and hem finishing. Stitches are cast on at the neck edge, with yarn over increases at the shoulder seams until the finished chest measurement is accomplished. At that point the sleeve stitches are put on holders while the body is knitted; finally, the sleeves are worked flat, to be sewn when the knitting is completed.

An easy pattern.

SIZES
Child: 2 (4, 6, 8, 10)
Adult: 34 (38, 42, 46, 50, 54)

GAUGE
18 sts & 22 rows = 4" (10 cm) in St st, on Size 7 needle

FINISHED MEASUREMENTS
Chest measurement: Child: 24 (26, 28, 30, 32)"/ 61 (66, 71, 76, 81.5) cm. **Adult:** 34 (38, 42, 46, 50, 54)"/86.5 (96.5, 106.5, 117, 127, 137) cm
Length to underarm: Child: 8½ (9½, 10½, 11½, 12½)"/ 21.5 (24, 26.5, 29, 32) cm. **Adult:** 14 (15, 16, 17, 17½, 18½)"/35.5 (38, 40.5, 43, 44.5, 47) cm
Sleeve to underarm: Child: 9 (10, 10½, 11, 12)"/ 23 (25.5, 26.5, 28, 30.5) cm. **Adult:** 16½ (18, 18½, 19, 20, 20)"/ 42 (45.5, 47, 48.5, 51, 51) cm

MATERIALS
Yarn
Double Twist or 2-Ply Wool: **Child:** 2 (2, 3, 3, 4) 4 oz skeins. **Adult:** 5 (5, 6, 7, 7, 7) 4 oz skeins
Mountain Mohair: **Child:** 3 (4, 5, 6, 7) 2 oz skeins. **Adult:** 8 (9, 10, 11, 12, 13) 2 oz skeins
Green Mountain Green: **Child:** 4 (5, 6, 7, 8) 2 oz skeins. **Adult:** 9 (11, 12, 13, 14, 15) 2 oz skeins

NEEDLES
Roll Neck Version
Sizes 5 (3.75 mm) & 7 (4.5 mm) 16" (40 cm) circular for all sweater sizes
Sizes 5 (3.75 mm) & 7 (4.5 mm) 29" (80 cm) circular for Sizes 8, 10, 34, 38, 42
Sizes 5 (3.75 mm) & 7 (4.5 mm) 36" (80 cm) circular for Sizes 46, 50, 54
Or sizes needed to obtain gauge.

Cable Neck Version
1 pair Size 5 (3.75 mm) straight needles for all sizes
Size 7 (4.5 mm) circular needles for sizes noted for Roll Neck Version
Or sizes needed to obtain gauge.

CABLE PATTERN
Round 1: *P1, k1, p1, k3, repeat from *.
Round 2: Same as Round 1.
Round 3: *P1, k1, p1, turn cable by skipping over 2 sts and knitting the third, leaving it on needle, knitting the 2 sts, then sliding the third st from needle, repeat from *.
Round 4: Same as Round 1.

BODY
Roll Neck Version: Using smaller 16" needle, **CAST ON** 66 (66, 66, 72, 72) sts for Child, 72 (78, 84, 84, 90, 96) sts for Adult. Join, being careful not to twist sts. Work in St st (knit all sts) for 1½ inches for Child, 2 inches for Adult. Then work k1, p1 ribbing for ¾ inch for Child, 1 inch for Adult. Knit

1 more round, dec 2 sts for Size 2, inc (2, 2, 0, 0) sts for other Child sizes, and inc 4 (2, 0, 4, 2, 0) sts for Adult sizes. This completes the neck edge.

Cable Neck Version: Using 16" needle, **CAST ON** 66 (66, 66, 72, 72) sts for Child, 72 (78, 84, 84, 90, 96) sts for Adult. Join sts

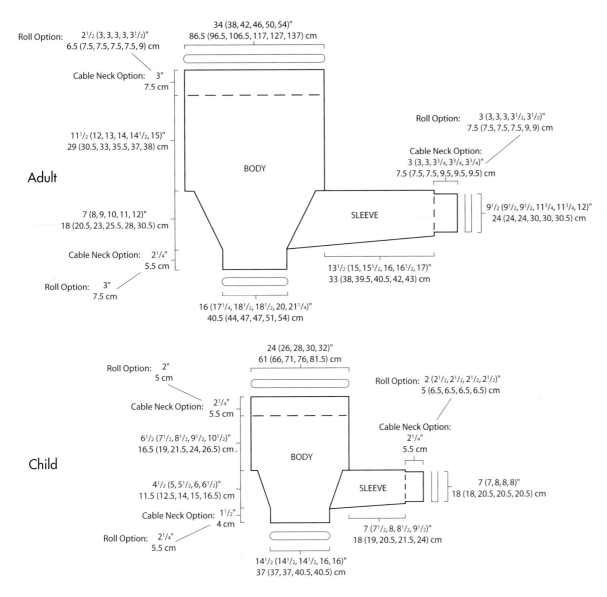

Adult

Roll Option: 2½ (3, 3, 3, 3, 3½)"
6.5 (7.5, 7.5, 7.5, 7.5, 9) cm

Cable Neck Option: 3"
7.5 cm

34 (38, 42, 46, 50, 54)"
86.5 (96.5, 106.5, 117, 127, 137) cm

11½ (12, 13, 14, 14½, 15)"
29 (30.5, 33, 35.5, 37, 38) cm

BODY

Roll Option: 3 (3, 3, 3, 3½, 3½)"
7.5 (7.5, 7.5, 7.5, 9, 9) cm

Cable Neck Option:
3 (3, 3, 3¾, 3¾, 3¾)"
7.5 (7.5, 7.5, 9.5, 9.5, 9.5) cm

SLEEVE

9½ (9½, 9½, 11¾, 11¾, 12)"
24 (24, 24, 30, 30, 30.5) cm

7 (8, 9, 10, 11, 12)"
18 (20.5, 23, 25.5, 28, 30.5) cm

Cable Neck Option: 2¼"
5.5 cm

Roll Option: 3"
7.5 cm

13½ (15, 15½, 16, 16½, 17)"
33 (38, 39.5, 40.5, 42, 43) cm

16 (17¼, 18½, 18½, 20, 21¼)"
40.5 (44, 47, 47, 51, 54) cm

Child

Roll Option: 2"
5 cm

Cable Neck Option: 2¼"
5.5 cm

24 (26, 28, 30, 32)"
61 (66, 71, 76, 81.5) cm

6½ (7½, 8½, 9½, 10½)"
16.5 (19, 21.5, 24, 26.5) cm

BODY

Roll Option: 2 (2½, 2½, 2½, 2½)"
5 (6.5, 6.5, 6.5, 6.5) cm

Cable Neck Option:
2¼"
5.5 cm

SLEEVE

7 (7, 8, 8, 8)"
18 (18, 20.5, 20.5, 20.5) cm

4½ (5, 5½, 6, 6½)"
11.5 (12.5, 14, 15, 16.5) cm

Cable Neck Option: 1½"
4 cm

Roll Option: 2¼"
5.5 cm

7 (7½, 8, 8½, 9½)"
18 (19, 20.5, 21.5, 24) cm

14½ (14½, 14½, 16, 16)"
37 (37, 37, 40.5, 40.5) cm

and work Cable Pattern 2 times for Child, 3 times for Adult. Then work Round 1.

Purl 1 round for Child sizes. In this round, dec 2 sts for Size 2; on the other sizes inc (2, 2, 0, 0) sts. For Adult sizes, p1 round, k1 round, p1 round, inc 4 (2, 0, 4, 2, 0) sts, evenly spaced, in the last round. This will

complete the neck edge. There are 64 (68, 68, 72, 72) sts for Child, 76 (80, 84, 88, 92, 96) sts for Adult.

Both Versions
Working on larger 16" needle and knitting all sts, begin raglan inc as follows:
Round 1(inc round): *Yarn over (this makes

the inc), pm on needle, k1, yo, k22 (23, 23, 24, 24) sts for Child's Front, 25 (26, 27, 28, 29, 30) sts for Adult's Front, yo, pm on needle, k1, yo, k8 (9, 9, 10, 10) sts for Child's sleeve, 11 (12, 13, 14, 15, 16) sts for Adult's sleeve, repeat from * for back and second sleeve. (The single knit sts between the yo's are seam sts.)
Round 2: Knit all sts, including the yo's.

Continue alternating these two rounds, inc before and after each marked st. *Always count sts at the end of every inc round; there should be 8 more sts each time.* On larger sizes, when there are too many sts for the 16" needle, change to the longer needle. Shaping is complete after a total of 13 (15, 17, 18, 20) inc rounds for Child, 21 (25, 28, 31, 34, 37) inc rounds for Adult. There are a total of 168 (188, 204, 216, 232) sts for Child, 244 (280, 308, 336, 364, 392) sts for Adult. Knit 1 more round.

DIVIDE SLEEVE FROM BODY
In the next round, divide sleeve sts from Body sts as follows: Knit seam st, knit across front 48 (53, 57, 60, 64) sts for Child, 67 (76, 83, 90, 97, 104) sts for Adult, knit seam st, put sts for first sleeve on holder; cast on 4 (4, 4, 6, 6) underarm sts for Child, 8 (8, 10, 12, 14, 16) underarm sts for Adult; knit seam st, knit across Back 48 (53, 57, 60, 64) sts for Child, 67 (76, 83, 90, 97, 104) sts for Adult, knit seam st; put second sleeve sts on holder; cast on 4 (4, 4, 6, 6) underarm sts for Child, 8 (8, 10, 12, 14, 16) underarm sts for Adult. Continue on the 108 (118, 126, 136, 144) sts for Child, 154

(172, 190, 208, 226, 244) sts for Adult, until the Body measures 6½ (7½, 8½, 9½, 10½) inches for Child, 11½ (12, 13, 14, 14½, 15) inches for Adult, or desired length from underarm to ribbing.

Roll Neck Version: Change to smaller needle. Work in k1, p1 ribbing for 2 inches for Child, 2½ (3, 3, 3, 3, 3½) inches for Adult. Bind off loosely in ribbing.

Cable Neck Version: Continuing on larger needle, k1 round, dec 0 (0, 2, 4, 0) st(s) for Child, 4 sts for Adult. There are 108 (120, 126, 132, 144) sts for Child, 150 (168, 186, 204, 222, 240) sts for Adult. Purl 1 round. *For Adult sizes only,* k1 round, p1 round. Work Cable Pattern 3 times for Child, 4 times for Adult. Bind off loosely.

SLEEVES

Transfer sleeve sts from holder to Size 7 needle. With RS facing, cast on 2 (2, 2, 3, 3) sts for Child, 4 (4, 5, 6, 7, 8) sts for Adult. Knit across sleeve sts, cast on 2 (2, 2, 3, 3) sts for Child, 4 (4, 5, 6, 7, 8) sts for Adult. There are a total of 38 (43, 47, 52, 56) sts for Child, 61 (70, 79, 88, 97, 106) sts for Adult.

Child: Work back and forth in St st (k1 row, p1 row), until sleeve measures 7 (7½, 8, 8½, 9½) inches, or desired length to cuff, ending

with a purl row. Next row, dec 7 (12, 10, 15, 19) sts evenly across row. There are 31 (31, 37, 37, 37) sts.

Adult: Work back and forth in St st (k1 row, p1 row), dec 1 st each end of row every 2½ (1½, 1¾, 1¼, 1, 1) inches for a total of 5 (8, 8, 12, 15, 16) times. There are 51 (54, 63, 64, 67, 74) sts. Work straight until sleeve measures 13½ (15, 15½, 16, 16½, 17) inches, or desired length to cuff, ending with a purl row. Next row, dec 8 (11, 20, 15, 18, 19) sts evenly across row. There are 43 (43, 43, 49, 49, 55) sts.

Roll Neck Version, *Child and Adult:* Change to smaller needle. Work in k1, p1 ribbing for 2 (2½, 2½, 2½, 2½) inches for Child, 3 (3, 3, 3, 3½, 3½) inches for Adult. Bind off loosely.

Cable Neck Version, *Child and Adult:* Change to smaller needle. Knit 1 row. Then, *for Adult sizes only,* k2 rows. Work Cable Pattern 3 times for Child, 4 times for Sizes 34–42, 5 times for Sizes 46–54. The Cable Pattern will be as follows:

CABLE PATTERN
Row 1: *P1, k1, p1, k3, repeat from *, end with p1.
Rows 2 & 4: K1, *p3, k1, p1, k1, repeat from *.

Row 3: *P1, k1, p1, turn cable, repeat from *, end with p1.
Bind off loosely.

FINISHING
Beginning at wrist, sew sleeve seams. Then join underarm Body sts to underarm sleeve sts. Weave in loose ends.

For washing instructions read "Caring for Handknits" on page xiv.

STAINED GLASS PULLOVER

(Adult model on page 11 pictured in Colorway 2, Child model on page 31 pictured in Colorway 1)

The Spinnery's signature sweater is easier to knit than it looks. Background and pattern colors change every three to six rows, creating gradual color shifts using only two colors at a time in most rows. Included in the directions are step-by-step instructions for knitting the sweater with "steeks," an age-old method of circular knitting. The garment is designed as a tube and knit in the round to the shoulders. Sleeve and neck openings are made later by cutting open the knitted steeks, the knitting equivalent of seam allowances. This quick, easy technique results in a beautifully crafted sweater and may completely change your approach to knitting multicolor patterns. A thorough discussion of steeks is included in "Using the Patterns" on page xv.

SIZES
Child: 4 (6, 8, 10, 12)
Adult: Petite (Small, Medium, Large, X-Large)

FINISHED MEASUREMENTS
Chest measurement: Child: 24 (26, 29, 31, 32)"/61 (66, 73.5, 78.5, 81.5) cm. **Adult:** 37 (40, 44, 48, 52)"/94 (101.5, 112, 122, 132) cm
Length to underarm: Child: 9 (9½, 10½, 11½, 12½)"/23 (24, 26.5, 29, 32) cm. **Adult:** 14 (16, 17, 17½, 18)"/35.5 (40.5, 43, 44.5, 45.5) cm
Length to shoulder: Child: 15 (16, 17½, 18½, 20)"/38 (40.5, 44.5, 47, 51) cm. **Adult:** 23 (26, 27½, 28, 29)"/58.5 (66, 70, 71, 73.5) cm
Sleeve length: Child: 12½ (13, 13½, 14½, 15½)"/32 (33, 34.5, 37, 39.5) cm. **Adult:** 19 (20, 21, 22, 23)"/48.5 (51, 53.5, 56, 58.5) cm

GAUGE
20 sts & 22 rows = 4" (10 cm) on Size 7 needle in St st with 2-color pattern

MATERIALS
Yarn: All colors are Mountain Mohair 2 oz skeins.
Needles
Size 5 (3.75 mm): 16" (40 cm) circular for all sizes
Size 6 (4.0 mm): 16" (40 cm) circular for all sizes
Size 7 (4.5 mm): set of 10" (25 cm) dpn for all sizes
Size 7 (4.5 mm): 16" (40 cm) circular for Sizes 4–6
Size 7 (4.5 mm): 29" (80 cm) circular for Sizes 8–Medium
Size 7 (4.5 mm): 36" (91.5 cm) circular for Sizes Large–X-Large
Or sizes needed to obtain gauge.
Tapestry needle
Stitch holder: 1 medium

BODY
CAST ON using the appropriate length Size 7 circular needle and Color A, 122 (130, 146, 154, 162) sts for Child, 186 (202, 218, 242, 258) sts for Adult. Making sure that the sts are not twisted on the needle, pm on needle, join sts, and work in Two-Color Rib as follows:

Two-Color Rib: Colorway 1 has a total of 4 rounds for Child, 8 rounds for Adult; Colorways 2 and 3 have 5 rounds for Child, 10 rounds for Adult.

*P1 Color A, k1 Color B, repeat from * to end of round (Child—1 round, Adult—2 rounds).

*P1 Color A, k1 Color C, repeat from * to end of round (Child—1 round, Adult—2 rounds).

*P1 Color A, k1 Color D, repeat from * to end of round (Child—1 round, Adult—2 rounds).

Colorways 2 & 3 only, work this round: *p1 Color A, k1 Color E, repeat from * to end of round (Child—1 round, Adult—2 rounds).

*p1 Color A, k1 Color F, repeat from * to end of round (Child—1 round, Adult—2 rounds).

BORDER PATTERN

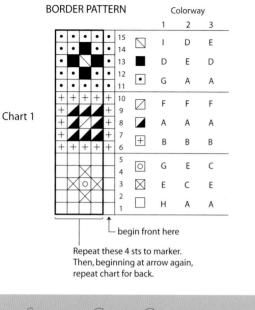

Chart 1

Colorway

symbol	1	2	3
◹	I	D	E
■	D	E	D
⊡	G	A	A
◸	F	F	F
◤	A	A	A
⊞	B	B	B
○	G	E	C
⊠	E	C	E
□	H	A	A

begin front here

Repeat these 4 sts to marker.
Then, beginning at arrow again,
repeat chart for back.

WINDOW PATTERN

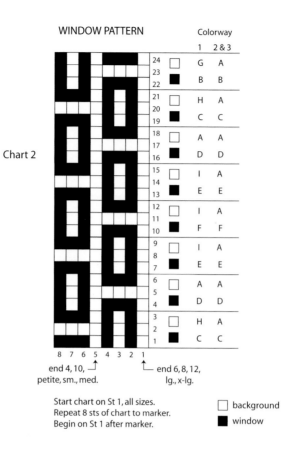

Chart 2

Colorway

symbol	1	2 & 3
□	G	A
■	B	B
□	H	A
■	C	C
□	A	A
■	D	D
□	I	A
■	E	E
□	I	A
■	F	F
□	I	A
■	E	E
□	A	A
■	D	D
□	H	A
■	C	C

end 4, 10,
petite, sm., med.

end 6, 8, 12,
lg., x-lg.

Start chart on St 1, all sizes.
Repeat 8 sts of chart to marker.
Begin on St 1 after marker.

□ background
■ window

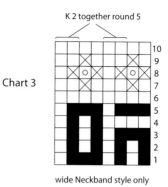

K 2 together round 5

Chart 3

wide Neckband style only

STAINED GLASS COLORWAYS

Colorway 1	CHILD	ADULT
A Peacock	2 (2, 2, 2, 2)	2 (3, 3, 3, 3)
B Raspberry	1 (1, 1, 1, 1)	1 (1, 2, 2, 2)
C Partridgeberry	1 (1, 1, 1, 1)	2 (2, 3, 3, 3)
D Rhubarb	1 (1, 1, 1, 1)	2 (2, 3, 3, 3)
E Coral Bell	1 (1, 1, 1, 1)	2 (2, 3, 3, 3)
F Day Lily	1 (1, 1, 1, 1)	1 (1, 2, 2, 2)
G Periwinkle	1 (1, 1, 1, 1)	1 (1, 2, 2, 2)
H Wintergreen	1 (1, 2, 2, 2)	2 (3, 3, 3, 3)
I Glacier Lake	1 (1, 2, 2, 2)	2 (3, 3, 3, 3)

Colorway 2		
A Midnight Blue	3 (3, 4, 4, 5)	6 (7, 8, 9, 10)
B Wintergreen	1 (1, 1, 1, 1)	1 (1, 2, 2, 2)
C Peacock	1 (1, 1, 1, 1)	2 (2, 3, 3, 3)
D Blue Gentian	1 (1, 1, 1, 1)	2 (2, 3, 3, 3)
E Lupine	1 (1, 1, 1, 1)	2 (2, 3, 3, 3)
F Glacier Lake	1 (1, 1, 1, 1)	1 (1, 2, 2, 2)

Colorway 3		
A Jet Black	3 (3, 4, 4, 5)	6 (7, 8, 9, 10)
B Midnight Blue	1 (1, 1, 1, 1)	1 (1, 2, 2, 2)
C Raven	1 (1, 1, 1, 1)	2 (2, 3, 3, 3)
D Alpine Shadow	1 (1, 1, 1, 1)	2 (2, 3, 3, 3)
E Grey Birch	1 (1, 1, 1, 1)	2 (2, 3, 3, 3)
F Edelweiss	1 (1, 1, 1, 1)	1 (1, 2, 2, 2)

Chart 1, Border Pattern: Change to St st and work Chart 1. On the first round, k61 (65, 73, 77, 81) sts for Child's Front, 93 (101, 109, 121, 129) sts for Adult's Front; pm on needle. Work across rem 61 (65, 73, 77, 81) sts for Child's Back, 93 (101, 109, 121, 129) sts for Adult's Back. Work all 15 rounds.

Chart 2, Window Pattern: Colorway 1, begin Chart 2 with Round 1. Colorways 2 & 3, work 1 round Color C and begin Chart 2 on Round 2.

All colorways, * work through Round 24, changing colors every 3 rounds as indicated. Then begin again at Round 1. Repeat from *. Continue working in this manner until entire piece measures 9 (9½, 10½, 11½, 12½) inches for Child, 14 (16, 17, 17½, 18) inches for Adult, or desired length to underarm. In following round, bind off first 3 (4, 4, 4, 4) sts for Child, 6 (7, 7, 7, 7) sts for Adult. Continuing in color pattern, work across Front to within 3 (4, 4, 4, 4) sts of marker for Child, 6 (7, 7, 7, 7) sts of marker for Adult; bind off 6 (8, 8, 8, 8) sts for Child, 12 (14, 14, 14, 14) sts for Adult. Continue across Back and bind off last 3 (4, 4, 4, 4) sts for Child, 6 (7, 7, 7, 7) sts for Adult. These bound off sts at each side of sweater mark the beginning of the armhole.

For all sizes, cast on 8 sts over the first set of bound off sts. Work across Front and cast on 8 sts over second set of bound off sts. There are now 126 (130, 146, 154, 162) sts for Child, 178 (190, 206, 230, 246) sts for Adult. In all rem rounds, these 2 sets of 8 sts are to be worked by alternating sts of the 2 colors; they make up the armhole steeks

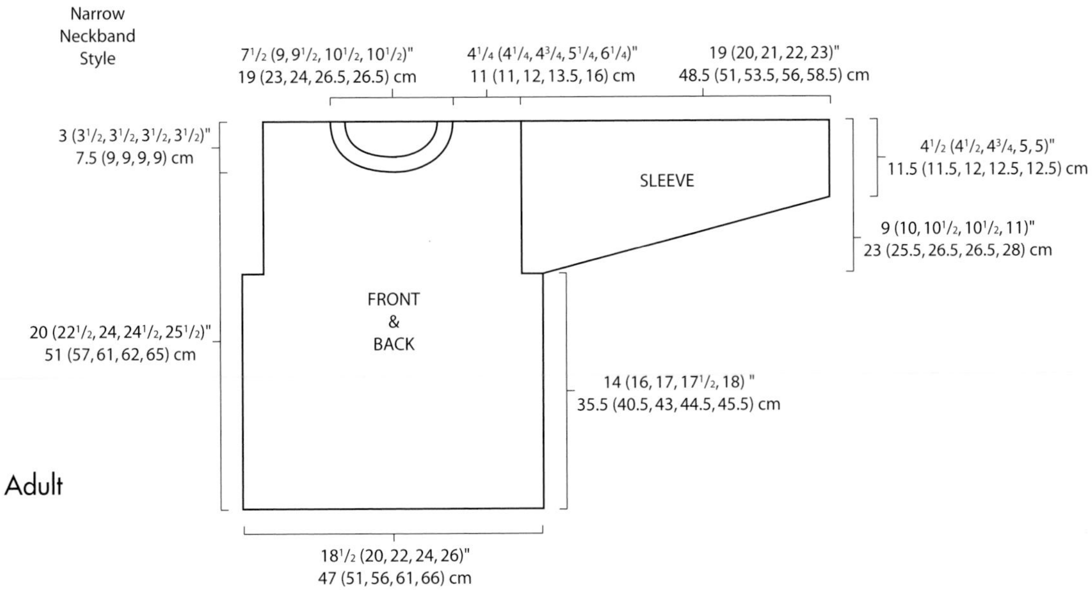
Narrow
Neckband
Style
7¹/₂ (9, 9¹/₂, 10¹/₂, 10¹/₂)"
19 (23, 24, 26.5, 26.5) cm
4¹/₄ (4¹/₄, 4³/₄, 5¹/₄, 6¹/₄)"
11 (11, 12, 13.5, 16) cm
19 (20, 21, 22, 23)"
48.5 (51, 53.5, 56, 58.5) cm
3 (3¹/₂, 3¹/₂, 3¹/₂, 3¹/₂)"
7.5 (9, 9, 9, 9) cm
SLEEVE
4¹/₂ (4¹/₂, 4³/₄, 5, 5)"
11.5 (11.5, 12, 12.5, 12.5) cm
9 (10, 10¹/₂, 10¹/₂, 11)"
23 (25.5, 26.5, 26.5, 28) cm
FRONT
&
BACK
20 (22¹/₂, 24, 24¹/₂, 25¹/₂)"
51 (57, 61, 62, 65) cm
14 (16, 17, 17¹/₂, 18)"
35.5 (40.5, 43, 44.5, 45.5) cm
18¹/₂ (20, 22, 24, 26)"
47 (51, 56, 61, 66) cm

Adult

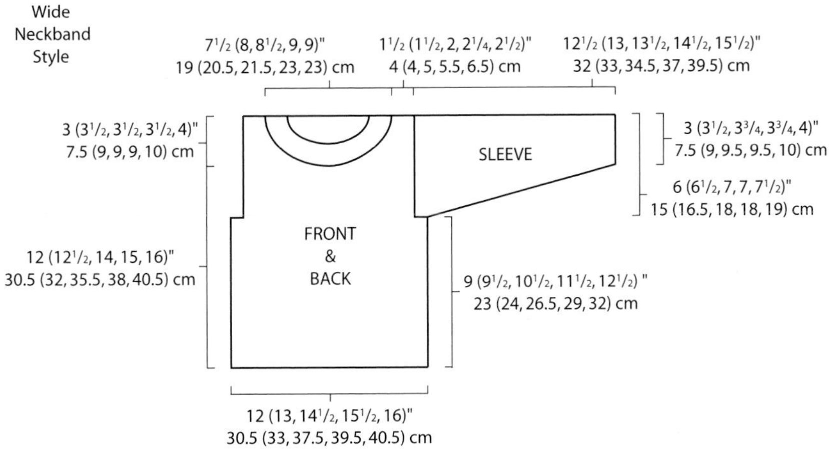
Wide
Neckband
Style
7¹/₂ (8, 8¹/₂, 9, 9)"
19 (20.5, 21.5, 23, 23) cm
1¹/₂ (1¹/₂, 2, 2¹/₄, 2¹/₂)"
4 (4, 5, 5.5, 6.5) cm
12¹/₂ (13, 13¹/₂, 14¹/₂, 15¹/₂)"
32 (33, 34.5, 37, 39.5) cm
3 (3¹/₂, 3¹/₂, 3¹/₂, 4)"
7.5 (9, 9, 9, 10) cm
SLEEVE
3 (3¹/₂, 3³/₄, 3³/₄, 4)"
7.5 (9, 9.5, 9.5, 10) cm
6 (6¹/₂, 7, 7, 7¹/₂)"
15 (16.5, 18, 18, 19) cm
FRONT
&
BACK
12 (12¹/₂, 14, 15, 16)"
30.5 (32, 35.5, 38, 40.5) cm
9 (9¹/₂, 10¹/₂, 11¹/₂, 12¹/₂)"
23 (24, 26.5, 29, 32) cm
12 (13, 14¹/₂, 15¹/₂, 16)"
30.5 (33, 37.5, 39.5, 40.5) cm

Child

where sleeves will later be added. The steeks will not be visible when sweater is complete. Except for these steek sts, maintain the pattern as before.

WIDE NECKBAND STYLE

Work until piece measures 3 (3, 3½, 3½, 3½) inches above beginning of armholes for Child, 5 (5½, 6, 6, 6½) inches above beginning of armholes for Adult. Knit across 25 (26, 29, 31, 32) sts of Front for Child, 36 (38, 42, 48, 51) sts of Front for Adult. Place next 13 (13, 15, 15, 17) sts on holder for Child, 17 (19, 19, 19, 21) sts on holder for Adult. These will later become the sts at the Front center of Neckband. Using the colors of this row, cast on 13 (13, 15, 15, 17) sts for Child, 17 (19, 19, 19, 21) sts for Adult, join sts, and continue to end of round. This is an unusual procedure, but stay with it!) In subsequent rounds work these cast on sts in Window Pattern. Continue working until armhole measures 6 (6½, 7, 7, 7½) inches for Child, 9 (10, 10½, 10½, 11) inches for Adult. Turn the entire piece WS out.

Shoulders: For first shoulder, *place 12 (12, 15, 16, 18) sts from Child's Front, 20 (22, 25, 30, 33) sts from Adult's Front on a straight needle; place corresponding sts from Back on a second straight needle, with points facing same direction. Join shoulder using Three Needle Bind Off method described in "Using the Patterns" on page xv. Repeat from * for second shoulder, leaving 39 (41, 43, 45, 45) sts between shoulders on both Front and Back for Child, 49 (51, 53, 55, 57) sts between shoulders on both Front and Back for Adult. Using tapestry needle, put these sts on a length of yarn so that the sweater can be laid out flat.

Neckband: Turn work RS out. To mark where sts will be picked up for Neckband, use tapestry needle and fine yarn or heavy thread of a color that will show up easily. Baste a curved line from sts on one side of holder to shoulder. Baste a corresponding curve on other side; continue this line across back of neck. The line at center Back should be 1 inch below shoulder level. Using Size 6 circular needle and color for first round of

Chart 1, begin at shoulder and pick up 1 st for each st in Body of sweater along basted line at back of neck; pick up and k5 sts per inch along basted line at side of neck front; knit sts from holder at center Front; continue picking up and knitting 5 sts per inch along basted line to shoulder.

Starting with back of neck, work Round 2 of Chart 1, beginning in such a way that the motif will be centered above the Window Pattern in Body of sweater. Continue to Front of sweater, increasing or decreasing a few sts if needed for the pattern to remain centered with "windows." Work Rounds 3 and 4 of chart 1. On Row 5 of Chart, dec as follows: *k2, k2tog, repeat from * to end of round. (Place the k2tog so that it falls between the small motifs. See Chart 3.) Work Two-Color Rib, working just 1 round of each color combination. Change to Size 5 16" circular needle. Using Color A, k1 round, p1 round, k6 rounds. In the following round, inc as follows: *k2, inc 1 in next st, repeat from * to end of round. Knit 4 rounds. Bind off loosely.

NARROW NECKBAND STYLE
Work until piece measures 4 (4, 4½, 4½, 4½) inches above beginning of armholes for Child, 6 (6½, 7, 7, 7½) inches above beginning of armholes for Adult. Knit across 19 (19, 23, 24, 26) sts of Front for Child, 29 (29, 33, 38, 42) sts of Front for Adult. Place next 25 (27, 27, 29, 29) sts on holder for Child, 31 (37, 37, 39, 39) sts on holder for

Stained Glass Pullover Colorway 1

Adult. These will later become the sts at the Front center of Neckband. Cast on 25 (27, 27, 29, 29) sts for Child, 31 (37, 37, 39, 39) sts for Adult, join sts, and continue to end of round. This is an unusual procedure, but stay with it! In subsequent rounds work these cast on sts in Window Pattern. Continue working until armhole measures 6 (6½, 7, 7, 7½) inches for Child, 9 (10, 10½, 10½, 11) inches for Adult. Turn the piece WS out.

Shoulders: For first shoulder, *place 16 (16, 19, 20, 21) sts from Child's Front, 25 (25, 27, 31, 35) sts from Adult's Front on a straight needle; place the corresponding sts from Back on a second straight needle, with points facing in the same direction. Join shoulders using the Three Needle Bind Off method. Repeat from * for second shoulder, leaving 31 (33, 35, 37, 39) sts between shoulders on both Front and Back for Child, 39 (45, 49, 53, 53) sts between shoulders on both Front and Back for Adult. Using tapestry needle, put Front sts on a length of yarn so that the sweater can be laid out flat.

Neckband: Turn the entire piece RS out. To mark where sts will be picked up for Neckband, use tapestry needle and fine yarn or heavy thread of a color that will show up easily. Baste a curved line from sts on one side of holder to shoulder. Baste a corresponding curve on other side. Using Size 6 circular needle and Color A, begin at shoulder and knit sts from needle at back of Neck; pick up and k5 sts per inch along basted line at side of neck Front; knit sts

from holder at center Front; continue picking up and knitting 5 sts per inch along basted line to shoulder. Work Two-Color Rib, working just 1 round of each color combination. Change to Size 5 16" circular needle. Using Color A, k1 round, p1 round, k6 rounds. Bind off loosely.

BOTH STYLES
Using sewing machine or small hand stitches, sew a double line of sts approximately ⅛ inch from picked up edge of Neckband. (These sts need to be behind the Neckband, not visible on RS of sweater.) This line of sewing secures the knitting. It is now safe to cut the extra fabric out from under the neckband! Using sharp scissors, cut to about ¼ inch from sewn line. Turn Neckband to inside along purl round and sew in place, covering the line of sewn sts and cut edge.

Sleeve: Using Color A and dpn, cast on 30 (34, 38, 38, 40) sts for Child, 44 (46, 48, 50, 52) sts for Adult. Divide sts onto 3 needles, being careful not to twist; join sts and work Two-Color Rib with just 1 round of each color combination. (In all, there will be 4 rounds for Colorway 1, 5 rounds Colorways 2 & 3.) Begin Chart 1, inc 7 (7, 7, 7, 9) sts for Child, 9 (11, 13, 11, 13) sts for Adult in first round. There are now 37 (41, 45, 45, 49) sts for Child, 53, (57, 61, 61, 65) sts for Adult. On Rounds 6 & 11 begin rounds with k1, inc 1; end rounds with inc 1, k1. After all 15 rounds have been worked, begin Chart 2. With each color change (every 3 rounds) continue to inc 1 st at beginning of round and 1 st at end of round for a total of 14 (14,

15, 15, 15) times for Child, 21 (24, 24, 24, 25) for Adult. There are 65 (69, 75, 75, 79) sts for Child, 95 (105, 109, 109, 115) sts for Adult. Work the first and last sts of each round in background color and work the increased sts into the Window Pattern.

When sleeve measures 11½ (12, 12½, 13½, 14½) inches for Child, 17½ (18½, 19½, 20½, 21½) inches for Adult, bind off the last st of round and then first st of next round. Cast on 6 sts over these bound off sts and then knit them as a steek, as done in the Body of sweater. When entire sleeve measures 12½ (13, 13½, 14½, 15½) inches for Child, 19 (20, 21, 22, 23) inches for Adult, or desired length, bind off all sts.

Sew a double line of small sts on each side of sleeve steek; cut steek down the center. Sew a double line of small sts on each side of armhole steek; cut steek down the center. Turn the resulting flaps to inside. Place folded edge of armhole over bound off edge of sleeve and sew in place; in the same way, join the folded edge of sleeve with bound off sts at bottom of armhole. Make second sleeve exactly the same.

FINISHING
Weave in loose ends.

For washing instructions read "Caring for Handknits" on page xiv.

Rosemary's Little & Middle-Sized
Sweaters & Green Mountain
Gardens Cardigan

ROSEMARY'S MIDDLE-SIZED SWEATER

(Pictured in Spice Mountain Mohair)

Cast on and follow the instructions for this one-color, very easy, very comfortable circular-knit pullover. Rosemary's cozy unisex sweater features a simple roll neck and cuffs, with a basic cable accent along the armhole and classic drop shoulders. The pattern is a perfect template for your own creative direction: Add stripes or texture to create an original.

An easy pattern.

Rosemary's Little & Middle Sweaters and Green Mountain Gardens—*Inspired by seasonal changes in the landscape, Designer Melissa Lumley created this steeked cardigan for children and adults in four distinctive colorways. Spinnery friend Rosemary Ladd's basic pullover design is both "Putney practical" and elegant made up in soft, lofty Mountain Mohair.*

SIZES
Small (Medium, Large)

FINISHED MEASUREMENTS
Chest: 40 (44, 48)"/101.5 (112, 122) cm
Length to shoulder: 24 (28, 32)"/61 (71, 81.5) cm

GAUGE
16 sts & 20 rows = 4" (10 cm)

MATERIALS
Yarn
Mountain Mohair: 8 (9, 9) 2 oz skeins
Green Mountain Green: 9 (10, 11) 2 oz skeins
Needles: Sizes 8 (5 mm) & 10 (6 mm) 29" (80 cm) circular; Sizes 8 (5 mm) & 10 (6 mm) 16" (40 cm) circular; Size 8 (5 mm) dpn, or sizes required for correct gauge; cable needle (cn)
Stitch holders: 3 medium

BODY
CAST ON 160 (176, 192) sts, using smaller circular 29" needle. Make sure sts are not twisted on needle. Join sts and work 1 inch in k1, p1 ribbing. Change to larger needle and work straight in St st (knit every round) for 15 (18½, 22½) inches, or 9 (9½, 9½) inches less than desired length to shoulder.

ARMHOLES FOR BACK
Knit across 80 (88, 96) sts for Back of sweater; place rem 80 (88, 96) sts for Front on long piece of yarn or large stitch holder.

Turn work and purl across Back.

Cable Pattern
Work Cable Pattern at beginning and end of each row as follows:
Row 1 (RS): K4, p1, k2, p1, k2, p1, k to within 11 sts of end of row, and p1, k2, p1, k2, p1, k4.
Row 2: P4, k1, p2, k1, p2, k1, p to within 11 sts of end of row, and k1, p2, k1, p2, k1, p4.
Row 3: Same as Row 1.
Row 4: Same as Row 2.
Row 5: K4, p1, sl 3 sts onto cn and hold in back of work, k2; p1, k2 from cn, p1, k to within 11 sts of end of row; p1, sl 2 sts onto cn and hold in front of work, k2, p1, k2 from cn, p1, k4.
Row 6: Same as Row 2.
Continue working in St st, with Cable Pattern at beginning and end of each row,

until armhole measures 9 (9½, 9½) inches, ending with a purl row. Work across 24 (28, 32) sts for right shoulder, and place these sts on holder; bind off 32 sts; work across last 24 (28, 32) sts for left shoulder and place these sts on second holder.

FRONT
Transfer sts for Front of sweater from holder onto needle, and work as for Back until armhole measures 5½ (6, 6½) inches, ending with a purl row.

To shape neck, k29 (33, 37) sts for Left Front and place these sts on holder; bind off the following 22 sts; k29 (33, 37) sts for Right Front. On each of the next 5 knit rows, dec 1 st at neck edge (beginning of row): k1, ssk, knit to end of row. Work additional rows, if needed, until length of Front measures same as Back. Place rem 24 (28, 32) sts on holder.

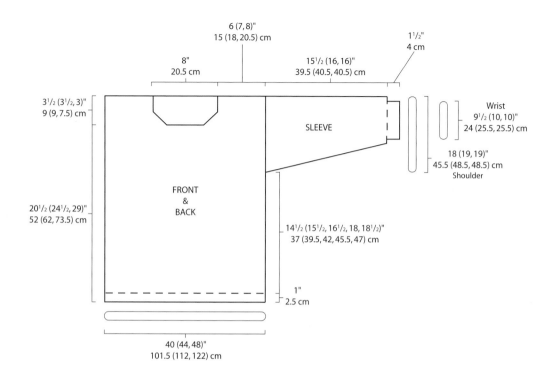

6 (7, 8)"
15 (18, 20.5) cm

1½"
4 cm

8"
20.5 cm

15½ (16, 16)"
39.5 (40.5, 40.5) cm

3½ (3½, 3)"
9 (9, 7.5) cm

SLEEVE

Wrist
9½ (10, 10)"
24 (25.5, 25.5) cm

18 (19, 19)"
45.5 (48.5, 48.5) cm
Shoulder

20½ (24½, 29)"
52 (62, 73.5) cm

FRONT
&
BACK

14½ (15½, 16½, 18, 18½)"
37 (39.5, 42, 45.5, 47) cm

1"
2.5 cm

40 (44, 48)"
101.5 (112, 122) cm

Transfer sts for Left Front onto needle. Work to correspond to Right Front by purling the first row. On the next 5 knit rows, work to last 3 sts, k2tog, k1. Continue straight until Left Front measures the same as the Right Front.

JOIN SHOULDERS
Turn sweater WS out. With RS together, join shoulders using Three Needle Bind Off method. Turn work RS out.

SLEEVES
With RS of work facing, using larger 16" needle and beginning at bottom of armhole, pick up and k36 (38, 38) sts along armhole edge to shoulder seam; pick up and k36 (38, 38) sts along Front armhole edge. There are now 72 (76, 76) sts. Place marker on needle, join sts, and work straight for 1 inch.

Decrease as follows: k1, sl 1, k1, psso, knit to within 3 sts of marker, k2tog, k1. Continue to dec in this manner every inch for a total of 14 (15, 15) times. There are 44 (46, 46) sts. Work straight until sleeve measures 15½ (16, 16) inches, or desired length to cuff. In next round *k5, k2tog, repeat from * 5 more times; knit to end of round. There are now 38 (40, 40) sts. Change to dpn and work k1, p1 ribbing for 1½ inches. Bind off loosely in ribbing.

Work second sleeve to correspond.

NECK
With RS of work facing, using smaller 16" needle and beginning at right shoulder seam, pick up and k32 sts for Back neck; pick up and k50 sts for Front neck. Work 4 rounds of k1, p1 ribbing; work 2 inches in St st. Bind off loosely.

FINISHING
Weave in loose ends.

For washing instructions read "Caring for Handknits" on page xiv.

ROSEMARY'S LITTLE SWEATER

(Pictured in Vincent's Gold Mountain Mohair on page 20)

By popular demand, here is the children's version of the Rosemary's Middle-Sized Sweater you already love to knit and wear. This cozy classic pullover is designed for all knitters to pick up and knit anywhere, anytime, and finish quickly. Make this up in Mountain Mohair and it will be enjoyed for several generations!

An easy pattern.

SIZES
2 (4, 6, 8, 10)

FINISHED MEASUREMENTS
Chest: 24 (26, 28, 30, 32)"/61 (66, 71, 76, 81.5) cm
Length to underarm: 8½ (9½, 10½, 11½, 12)"/21.5 (24, 26.5, 29, 30.5) cm
Length to shoulder: 13½ (15, 16½, 18, 19)"/34.5 (38, 42, 45.5, 48.5) cm
Sleeve: 9 (9½, 11, 12, 12)"/23 (24, 28, 30.5, 30.5) cm

GAUGE
16 sts & 20 rows = 4" (10 cm) in St st

MATERIALS
Yarn
Mountain Mohair: 3 (4, 4, 5, 6) 2 oz skeins
Needles: Sizes 8 (5.0 mm) & 9 (5.5 mm) 24" (60 cm) circular; 1 set each Size 8 (5.0 mm) & 9 (5.5 mm) dpn, or sizes required to obtain gauge; 1 pair straight needles any size; cable needle (cn)
Stitch holders: 1 large, 3 medium

BODY

CAST ON 96 (104, 112, 120, 128) sts, using smaller circular needle. Make sure sts are not twisted on the needle. Join sts and work ½ inch in k1, p1 ribbing. Change to larger needle and work in St st (knit each round) until piece measures 8½ (9½, 10½, 11½, 12) inches, or 5 (5½, 6, 6½, 7) inches less than desired length to shoulder. Divide for armholes by knitting 48 (52, 56, 60, 64) sts. Place these sts on large holder for Front.

BACK

Knit the rem sts. Turn work and purl back. Then work Cable Pattern at beginning and end of each row as follows:

Cable Pattern, Sizes 2, 4 & 6

Row 1 (RS): K2, p1, k1, p1, k1, p1, k to

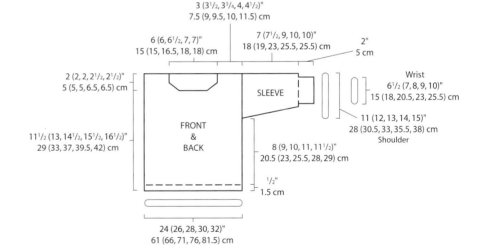

3 (3½, 3¾, 4, 4½)"
7.5 (9, 9.5, 10, 11.5) cm

6 (6, 6½, 7, 7)"
15 (15, 16.5, 18, 18) cm

7 (7½, 9, 10, 10)"
18 (19, 23, 25.5, 25.5) cm

2"
5 cm

2 (2, 2, 2½, 2½)"
5 (5, 5, 6.5, 6.5) cm

SLEEVE

Wrist
6½ (7, 8, 9, 10)"
15 (18, 20.5, 23, 25.5) cm

11½ (13, 14½, 15½, 16½)"
29 (33, 37, 39.5, 42) cm

FRONT & BACK

11 (12, 13, 14, 15)"
28 (30.5, 33, 35.5, 38) cm
Shoulder

8 (9, 10, 11, 11½)"
20.5 (23, 25.5, 28, 29) cm

½"
1.5 cm

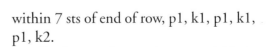

24 (26, 28, 30, 32)"
61 (66, 71, 76, 81.5) cm

within 7 sts of end of row, p1, k1, p1, k1, p1, k2.

Row 2: P2, k1, p1, k1, p1, k1, p to within 7 sts of end of row, k1, p1, k1, p1, k1, p2.

Row 3: K2, p1, sl 1 st onto cn and hold in

front of work, k1, p1, then k1 from cn, p1; knit to within 7 sts of end of row; p1, sl 2 sts onto cn and hold in back of work, k1, then (p1, k1) from cn, p1, k2.

Row 4: Same as Row 2.

Cable Pattern, Sizes 8 & 10

Row 1 (RS): K4, p1, k2, p1, k2, p1, k to within 11 sts of end of row, p1, k2, p1, k2, p1, k4.

Row 2: P4, k1, p2, k1, p2, k1, p to within 11 sts of end of row, k1, p2, k1, p2, k1, 4.

Row 3: Same as Row 1.

Row 4: Same as Row 2.

Row 5: K4, p1, slip 3 sts onto cn and hold in back of work, k2, then p1, k2 from cn, p1, knit to within 11 sts of end of row, p1, slip 2 sts onto cn and hold in front of work, k2, p1, then k2 from cn, p1, k4.

Row 6: Same as Row 2.

All sizes: Continue working in St st (k1 row, p1 row), with Cable Pattern at beginning and end of each row, until armhole measures 5 (5½, 6, 6½, 7) inches, ending with a WS row. On the following row, k12 (14, 15, 16, 18) sts for shoulder; bind off 24 (24, 26, 28, 28) sts for Back neck: k12 (14, 15, 16, 18) sts for second shoulder. Place shoulder sts on holders.

FRONT

Transfer sts from holder to needle, work as for Back until Front measures 3 (3½, 4, 4, 4½) inches, ending with a WS row. On the following row, work 17 (19, 20, 21, 23) sts for shoulder and place these sts on a small holder for Left Front shoulder; bind off 14 (14, 16, 18, 18) sts for Front neck; work rem sts for Right Front shoulder. On each of the next 5 knit rows, dec 1 st at neck edge (beginning of row): knit l, ssk, knit to end of row. There are 12 (14, 15, 16, 18) sts rem for shoulder. Continue until Right Front measures same as Back. Place these sts on a small holder. Work Left Front shoulder to correspond, making dec on RS rows: knit to last three sts, k2tog, k1.

JOIN SHOULDERS

Turn sweater WS out. Join shoulders using the Three Needle Bind Off method. Turn work RS out.

NECK

Using smaller dpn and beginning at right shoulder seam, pick up and k24 (24, 26, 28, 28) bound off sts for Back neck; pick up and k10 (10, 10, 12, 12) sts for side neck; pick up and k14 (14, 16, 18, 18) bound off sts at Front neck; pick up and k10 (10, 10, 12, 12) sts for side neck. Knit 2 rounds, then work 2 rounds of k1, p1 ribbing; then knit 4 rounds. Bind off loosely.

SLEEVE

Beginning at underarm and using larger dpn, pick up and k22 (24, 26, 28, 30) sts to shoulder seam; pick up and knit the same number of sts from the shoulder seam to underarm. There are now 44 (48, 52, 56, 60) sts. Work in St st for 1½ (2, 2, 2, 2) inches and then begin decreasing.

Round 1: Work to last 3 sts, k2tog, k1.

Round 2: Knit 1, k2tog, knit to end of round. Decrease every inch 4 (4, 7, 8, 6) times. Then decrease every ½ inch 3 (3, 0, 0, 3) times. There are now 30 (34, 38, 40, 42) sts. Work straight until sleeve measures 7 (7½, 9, 10, 10) inches, or 2 inches less than desired length. Decrease evenly in next round 2 (4, 4, 4, 4) times. Change to smaller dpn. Knit 2 rounds. Work 2 rounds k1, p1 ribbing. Knit 4 rounds. Bind off loosely.

FINISHING

Weave in loose ends.

For washing instructions read "Caring for Handknits" on page xiv.

GREEN MOUNTAIN GARDENS CARDIGAN

(Child model on page 20 pictured in "Poppies and Pansies" colorway; Adult model on page 51 pictured in "Mosses and Berries" colorway)

Designer Melissa Lumley's inspiration for this multipatterned, steeked cardigan was the many moods of the Vermont landscape. The "Poppies and Pansies" colorway evokes the bright flowers of late spring. "Daisies and Delphiniums" reflects the cool blues, purples, and white accents of a summer flower bed. "Mosses and Berries" captures the rich colors of autumn. "Winter Woods" mirrors the subtle shades of woodland in late November. Step-by-step directions in this pattern for knitting steeks introduce this simple technique for knitting a multicolor pattern quickly and easily. A thorough discussion of steeks is included in "Using the Patterns" on page xv.

An advanced pattern.

SIZES
Child: Small (Medium, Large)
Adult: Small (Medium, Large)

FINISHED MEASUREMENTS
Chest: Child: 30 (33, 35½)"/76 (84, 90) cm.
   Adult: 39¼ (44¾, 50½)"/99.5 (113.5, 128.5) cm
These measurements include the Front Band, which adds 1½" (4.0 cm) to the Child's sweater, 2¼" (5.5 cm) to the Adult's sweater.
Length to shoulder: Child: 15¼ (19¾, 23¼)"/38.5 (50, 59) cm.
   Adult: 24¼"/61.5 cm all sizes
Sleeve: Child: 12 (14¼, 17½)"/30.5 (36, 44.5) cm. **Adult:** 18½"/47 cm all sizes

GAUGE
20 sts & 24 rows = 4" (10 cm) on Size 7 (4.5 mm) needles

MATERIALS
Yarn
Mountain Mohair: 2 oz skeins
Needles
Sizes 3, 5 & 7 (3.25, 3.75 & 4.5 mm) dpn for sleeves
Sizes 3, 5 & 7 (3.25, 3.75 & 4.5 mm) 24" (60 cm) circular for Child
Sizes 3, 5 & 7 (3.25, 3.75 & 4.5 mm) 29" (80 cm) circular for Adult
Size 7 (4.5 mm) 16" (40 cm) circular for larger size sleeves
Or sizes required for correct gauge.
Clasps: Child: Size Small: 6 small (1¾" x ⅞"/4.5 x 7.5 cm); Medium & Large: 8, 10 medium (1¾" x ⅝"/4.5 x 1.6 cm). **Adult,** all sizes: 8 large (2" x ¾"/5.0 x 2.0 cm)

BODY
With Size 3 circular needle and first color in Chart 1, **CAST ON** 145 (159, 173) sts for Child, 187 (215, 243) sts for Adult. Work 6 rows in St st. Work Picot hem row as follows:

Picot hem: K1 *yo, k2tog* repeat from * to * to end of row.
Change to Size 5 needle and work first 3 rows of Chart 1 in St st. At the end of Row 3, cast on 5 sts for center Front steek. Join sts, making sure they are not twisted. Place markers on each side of steek sts. Begin following all charts on first st after pm.
NB: To lengthen Body, add solid MC rows at the beginning and end of charts. Adult Body can be lengthened by repeating Chart 9, and then Chart 6 after working Charts 12 and 6. Remember to adjust neck and armhole location accordingly. Join new colors at center of steek. Work steek in alternate sts of background and pattern colors, beginning and ending with background. Complete Chart 1. Change to Size 7 needle. Follow charts until sweater measures 8¼ (11¾, 14¼) inches for Child, 14½ inches for Adult, or desired length to underarm.

ARMHOLES
After working steek sts, work 32 (36, 39) sts for Child, 46 (53, 60) sts for Adult, and bind off 8 sts for Child, 2 sts for Adult for armhole. Work 65 (71, 79) sts for Child, 91

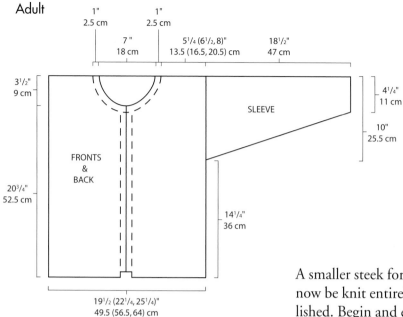

Adult

1" 2.5 cm   1" 2.5 cm

7" 18 cm   5¼ (6½, 8)" 13.5 (16.5, 20.5) cm   18½" 47 cm

3½" 9 cm

SLEEVE

4¼" 11 cm

10" 25.5 cm

FRONTS & BACK

20¾" 52.5 cm

14¼" 36 cm

19½ (22¼, 25¼)" 49.5 (56.5, 64) cm

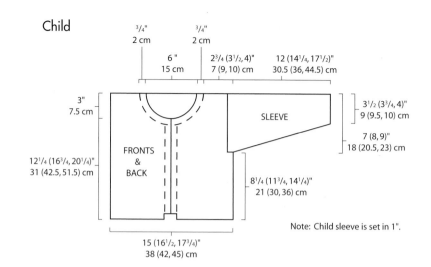

Child

¾" 2 cm   ¾" 2 cm

6" 15 cm   2¾ (3½, 4)" 7 (9, 10) cm   12 (14¼, 17½)" 30.5 (36, 44.5) cm

3" 7.5 cm

SLEEVE

3½ (3¾, 4)" 9 (9.5, 10) cm

7 (8, 9)" 18 (20.5, 23) cm

FRONTS & BACK

12¼ (16¾, 20¼)" 31 (42.5, 51.5) cm

8¼ (11¾, 14¼)" 21 (30, 36) cm

Note: Child sleeve is set in 1".

15 (16½, 17¾)" 38 (42, 45) cm

(105, 119) sts for Adult, for Back, bind off 8 sts for Child, 2 sts for Adult, for second armhole. Work 32 (36, 39) sts for Child, 46 (53, 60) sts for Adult. On following round, cast on 8 sts for Child, 2 sts for Adult, for armhole steek. To help maintain pattern alignment, continue to follow charts when working these steek sts. Work until Body measures 12¼ (16¾, 20¼) inches for Child, 20¾ inches for Adult.

NECK Shaping

Break yarns in use. For Child, slip center Front steek and 6 sts on each side on holder for neck; for Adult, slip center Front steek and 10 sts on either side on holder for neck. Join yarns at neck edge and work round. Cast on 6 sts for Child, 10 sts for Adult; pm on needle, cast on 6 sts for Child, 10 sts for Adult. Center Front steek sts have been eliminated.

A smaller steek for the neck opening will now be knit entirely in pattern as established. Begin and end rounds at marker now, maintaining patterns as before. When Body measures 15¼ (19¾, 23¼) inches for Child, 24¼ inches for Adult, or desired length, with MC k31 (35, 38) sts for Child, 45 (52, 59) sts for Adult, bind off 10 sts for Child, 4 sts for Adult over armhole steek; k63 (69, 77) sts for Child, k89 (103, 117) sts for Adult for Back; bind off 10 sts for Child, 4 sts for Adult over second armhole; k31 (35, 38) sts for Child, k45 (52, 59) sts for Adult. Slip Right Front sts onto a spare circular needle, Left Front onto another.

SEW STEEKS

With thread that matches MC, sew 2 rows of small sts by hand or, preferably, sewing machine on right and left sides of center Front steek st and on right and left sides of center above neck. With sharp scissors, cut open the Front between the two lines of sts. Repeat procedure on armhole steeks.

JOIN SHOULDERS

Turn sweater ws out. Using the Three Needle Bind Off method, starting at armhole edges, join 17 (20, 24) sts for Child, 27 (34, 41) sts for Adult. Leave rem Back sts on needle for neck; slip rem Front sts on holders.

Front Band: With Size 5 needle and first color in Chart 2, with RS facing, beginning on fourth row above Picot hem row, pick up 3 sts for every 4 rows along Front, working between first and second sts of charted pattern. With WS facing, k1 row to form ridge. Change to MC. On Child sweater, work 3 rows in St st, change to Size 3 needle, k1 row with WS facing, work 3 rows in St st. Bind off sts. Repeat on other side of Front. For Adult Front Band, after garter ridge, in St st work 2 rows MC, 1 row of alternate sts of main color and first color in Chart 1, then 3 rows of first color in Chart 1. Change to Size 3 needle, p1 row with RS facing, work 6

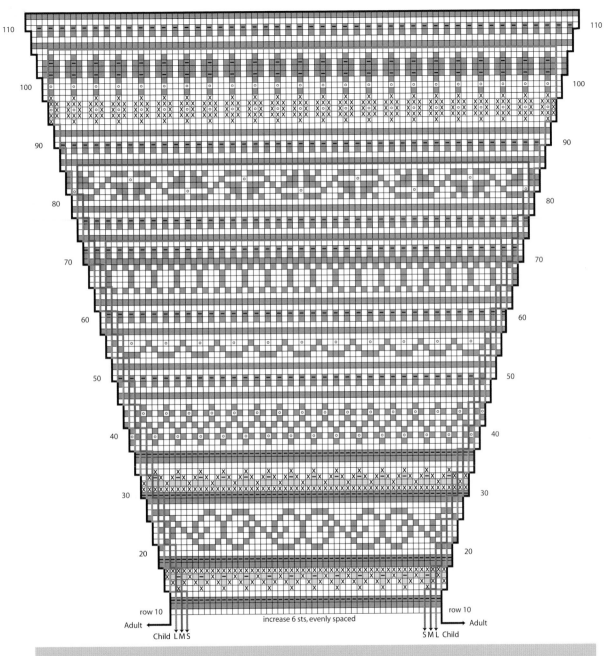

SLEEVE CHART

To keep yarns from tangling and to help make the knitting even, use the colors in a consistent order. Holding and using the background color on top and the second color underneath will make the pattern stand out more. When a third color is added, hold it beneath the second color.

GREEN MOUNTAIN GARDENS COLORWAYS

Poppies & Pansies

YARN NAME	CHILD Sm (Med, Lg)	ADULT Sm (Med, Lg)
Blue Violet (MC)	2 (3, 3)	4 (4, 4)
Partridgeberry (2nd)	1 (2, 2)	3 (4, 4)
Vincent's Gold	1 (1, 1)	1 (1, 1)
Day Lily	1 (1, 1)	1 (1, 1)
Coral Bell	1 (1, 1)	1 (1, 1)
Rhubarb	1 (1, 1)	2 (2, 2)
Raspberry	1 (1, 1)	1 (1, 1)
Glacier Lake	1 (1, 1)	2 (3, 3)
Wintergreen	1 (1, 1)	2 (2, 2)
Peacock	1 (2, 2)	2 (2, 2)

Daisies & Delphiniums

YARN NAME	CHILD Sm (Med, Lg)	ADULT Sm (Med, Lg)
Glacier Lake (MC)	2 (3, 3)	4 (4, 4)
Edelweiss (2nd)	2 (3, 3)	4 (4, 5)
Ice Blue	1 (1, 1)	1 (1, 1)
Sky Blue	1 (1, 1)	1 (1, 1)
Lupine	1 (1, 1)	2 (3, 3)
Blue Gentian	1 (1, 1)	2 (2, 2)
Wintergreen	1 (1, 1)	1 (2, 2)

Mosses & Berries

YARN NAME	CHILD Sm (Med, Lg)	ADULT Sm (Med, Lg)
Jet Black (MC)	2 (3, 3)	4 (4, 4)
Claret (2nd)	1 (2, 2)	3 (4, 4)
Rhubarb	1 (1, 1)	1 (1, 1)
Raspberry	1 (1, 1)	1 (1, 2)
Elderberry	1 (1, 1)	1 (1, 1)
Midnight Blue	1 (1, 1)	2 (2, 2)
Moss	1 (1, 1)	2 (3, 3)
Balsam	1 (1, 1)	1 (2, 2)

Winter Woods

YARN NAME	CHILD Sm (Med, Lg)	ADULT Sm (Med, Lg)
Raven (MC)	2 (3, 3)	4 (4, 4)
Lupine (2nd)	2 (3, 3)	4 (4, 5)
Blizzard	1 (1, 1)	2 (3, 3)
Ice Blue	1 (1, 1)	2 (3, 3)
Blue Gentian	1 (1, 1)	1 (1, 1)
Concord Grape	1 (1, 1)	1 (1, 1)
Alpine Shadow	1 (1, 1)	2 (2, 2)
Balsam	1 (2, 2)	2 (2, 2)

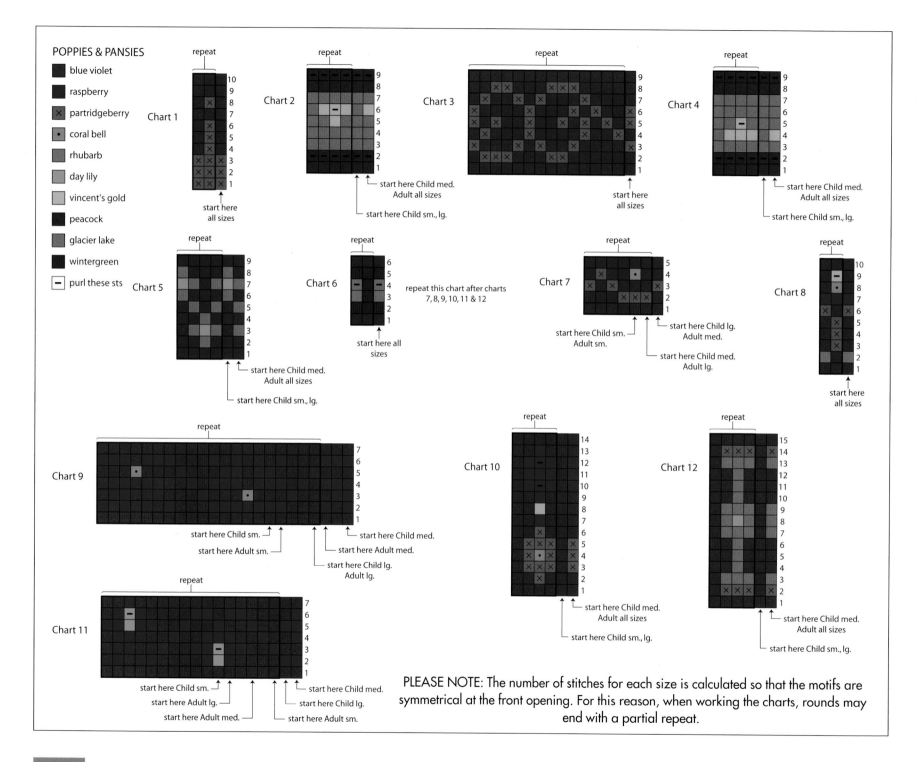

POPPIES & PANSIES

- blue violet
- raspberry
- partridgeberry
- coral bell
- rhubarb
- day lily
- vincent's gold
- peacock
- glacier lake
- wintergreen
- — purl these sts

Chart 1 — start here all sizes

Chart 2 — start here Child med. Adult all sizes — start here Child sm., lg.

Chart 3 — start here all sizes

Chart 4 — start here Child med. Adult all sizes — start here Child sm., lg.

Chart 5 — start here Child med. Adult all sizes — start here Child sm., lg.

Chart 6 — repeat this chart after charts 7, 8, 9, 10, 11 & 12 — start here all sizes

Chart 7 — start here Child sm. Adult sm. — start here Child lg. Adult med. — start here Child med. Adult lg.

Chart 8 — start here all sizes

Chart 9 — start here Child sm. — start here Adult sm. — start here Child med. — start here Adult med. — start here Child lg. Adult lg.

Chart 10 — start here Child med. Adult all sizes — start here Child sm., lg.

Chart 12 — start here Child med. Adult all sizes — start here Child sm., lg.

Chart 11 — start here Child sm. — start here Adult lg. — start here Adult med. — start here Child med. — start here Child lg. — start here Adult sm.

PLEASE NOTE: The number of stitches for each size is calculated so that the motifs are symmetrical at the front opening. For this reason, when working the charts, rounds may end with a partial repeat.

28

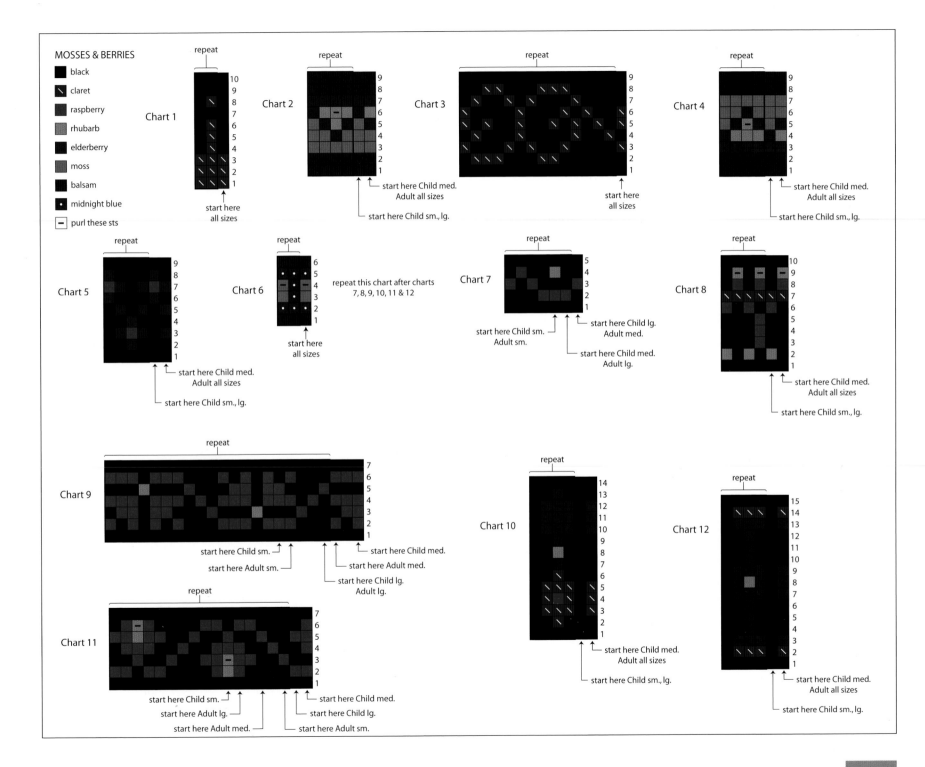

MOSSES & BERRIES

- black
- claret
- raspberry
- rhubarb
- elderberry
- moss
- balsam
- midnight blue
- — purl these sts

rows in St st. Bind off sts. Fold Front Band to inside over steek and stitch down.

NECK

With Size 5 circular needle and first color in Chart 2, pick up 4 sts for Child, 6 sts for Adult, along top edge of Front Band. Knit 6 sts for Child, 10 sts for Adult, from holder. Move up 1 row, pick up 1 st through st in Body, continue moving up and over 1 row and 1 st, picking up 1 st for each row, until 9 sts for Child and 8 sts for Adult have been picked up. Turn and pick up 3 sts for every 4 rows in a straight line to shoulder. Knit Back neck sts, repeat pick up procedure to Front Band. With WS facing, knit 1 row to form garter ridge. For Child, change to MC, work 6 rows in St st. Bind off sts. For Adult, work neck as for Front Band. After binding off sts, sew 2 rows of small hand or machine sts next to picked up neck sts. Adult Neckband will hide the steek: Fold Neckband over and stitch down. Child Neckband does not hide the steek: Trim steek and hand stitch it down carefully.

SLEEVES

With Size 3 dpn and first color in Chart 1, cast on 36 (38, 40) sts for Child, 42 sts for Adult. Join sts, making sure they are not twisted on needles. Place marker at beginning of round. Knit 6 rounds. Work Picot hem round. Change to Size 5 needles, work Chart 1. In last row of chart, inc 6 sts evenly spaced. There are now 42 (44, 46) sts for Child and 48 sts for Adult. Change to Size 7 needles. Follow charts, referring to sleeve chart for alignment. At the same time, inc 1 st on each side of pm every 4 rounds until there are 70 (80, 90) sts for Child, 100 sts for Adult. When there are sufficient sts, change to 16" Size 7 circular needle. *NB: To lengthen sleeves, add solid MC rows at the beginning and end of charts.*

Child: When sleeve measures 1 inch less than 11 (13¼, 16½) inches or desired length, bind off first and last st of round, cast on 2 sts over bound off sts on the following round for underarm steek. Complete sleeve. With MC, bind off sts. Sew steek as for armhole, cut open in center. Sew sleeve into armhole, forming right angle at bottom corners. **Adult:** When Adult sleeve is 18½ inches or desired length, bind off with MC. Sew into armhole.

FINISHING

Fold sleeve and bottom hems to inside on Picot hem row and stitch in place. Weave in ends, sew on clasps.

For washing instructions read "Caring for Handknits" on page xiv.

Green Mountain Gardens cardigan: Mosses and Berries colorway

Puntas & Stained Glass—An Andean knitting technique lends a decorative touch to a cap and basic drop-shoulder pullover for children and adults. Designer Melissa Lumley offers an exuberant segue of color in the Stained Glass Pullover.

Puntas Sweater, Punta Edged Cap &
Stained Glass Pullover

PUNTAS SWEATER

(Child model on page 31 pictured in Rhubarb Mountain Mohair)

This pullover's easy-to-learn decorative three-color edge of *puntas* (points) is inspired by Cynthia LeCount's book, *Andean Folk Knitting*. The sweater is worked in the round to the armholes. In classic drop-shoulder fashion, the sleeve stitches are picked up at the armhole and worked in the round to the cuff, eliminating the need for sewing up seams.

An easy pattern.

SIZES
Child: 2 (4, 6, 8, 10)
Adult: 34 (38, 42, 46, 50)

FINISHED MEASUREMENTS
Chest: Child: 24 (26, 28, 30, 32)"/61 (66, 71, 76, 81.5) cm. Adult: 34 (38, 42, 46, 50)"/86.5 (96.5, 106.5, 117, 127) cm.
Length to underarm: Child: 8½ (9½, 10½, 11½, 12)"/21.5 (24, 26.5, 29, 30.5) cm. Adult: 14½ (15½, 16½, 18, 18½)"/37 (39.5, 42, 45.5, 47) cm.
Length to shoulder: Child: 13½ (15, 16½, 18, 19)"/34.5 (38, 42, 45.5, 48.5) cm. Adult: 23 (25, 26½, 28, 29½)"/58.5 (63.5, 67.5, 71, 75) cm.
Sleeve to underarm: Child: 9 (9½, 11, 12, 12)"/23 (24, 28, 30.5, 30.5) cm. Adult: 15½ (16½, 17½, 17½, 18)"/39.5 (42, 44.5, 44.5, 45.5) cm.

GAUGE
16 sts & 20 rows = 4" (10 cm)

MATERIALS
Yarn
Mountain Mohair: 2 oz skeins
Main Color (MC): **Child:** 4 (4, 4, 5, 6). **Adult:** 8 (9, 10, 11, 12)
Colors A & B: 1 2 oz skein each, all sizes
Needles
Child: Size 9 (5.5 mm) 24" (60 cm) circular
Adult: Size 9 (5.5 mm) 29/36" (80 cm) circular
All sizes: 1 set each Sizes 9 (5.5 mm) & 8 (5 mm) dpn
Or sizes required for correct gauge.
1 pair straight needles any size
Stitch holders: 1 large, 3 medium

BODY
CAST ON 168 (182, 196, 210, 224) sts for Child, 238 (266, 294, 322, 350) sts for Adult, using circular needle and Color A. Join sts, making sure sts are not twisted on needle, k1 st, and pm on needle. Each round begins with the st after this marker. With Color B, k1 round.

Puntas
NB: Puntas are begun with a multiple of 7 sts. When complete, a multiple of 4 sts remains.

Using MC, work as follows: *k4 sts. Slide the last 2 of these 4 sts back onto left needle and knit them together (one dec made). K1; pick up the second and third sts from right needle and slip them over the first st (one double dec has been made). Knit 2 sts. This completes one *punta,* which now has 4 sts. Repeat from * to end of round. There are now 96 (104, 112, 120, 128) sts for Child, 136 (152, 168, 184, 200) sts for Adult. Continuing in MC, work in St st (knit all rounds) until entire piece measures 8½ (9½, 10½, 11½, 12) inches for Child, 14½ (15½,

16½, 18, 18½) inches for Adult.

DIVIDE FOR ARMHOLES
Knit 48 (52, 56, 60, 64) sts for Child, 68 (76, 84, 92, 100) sts for Adult. Place these sts on holder for Front.

BACK
Cast on 1 st, knit the rem sts, cast on 1 st. There are now 50 (54, 58, 62, 66) sts for Child, 70 (78, 86, 94, 102) sts for Adult, for Back. Purl 1 row. Then continue in St st (k1 row, p1 row) until armhole measures

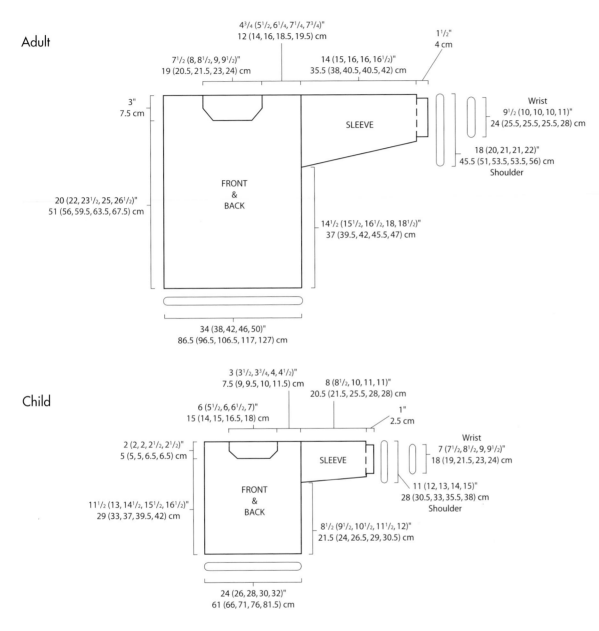

Adult

4³/₄ (5¹/₂, 6¹/₄, 7¹/₄, 7³/₄)"
12 (14, 16, 18.5, 19.5) cm

7¹/₂ (8, 8¹/₂, 9, 9¹/₂)"
19 (20.5, 21.5, 23, 24) cm

14 (15, 16, 16, 16¹/₂)"
35.5 (38, 40.5, 40.5, 42) cm

1¹/₂"
4 cm

3"
7.5 cm

SLEEVE

Wrist
9¹/₂ (10, 10, 10, 11)"
24 (25.5, 25.5, 25.5, 28) cm

18 (20, 21, 21, 22)"
45.5 (51, 53.5, 53.5, 56) cm
Shoulder

20 (22, 23¹/₂, 25, 26¹/₂)"
51 (56, 59.5, 63.5, 67.5) cm

FRONT
&
BACK

14¹/₂ (15¹/₂, 16¹/₂, 18, 18¹/₂)"
37 (39.5, 42, 45.5, 47) cm

34 (38, 42, 46, 50)"
86.5 (96.5, 106.5, 117, 127) cm

Child

3 (3¹/₂, 3³/₄, 4, 4¹/₂)"
7.5 (9, 9.5, 10, 11.5) cm

8 (8¹/₂, 10, 11, 11)"
20.5 (21.5, 25.5, 28, 28) cm

6 (5¹/₂, 6, 6¹/₂, 7)"
15 (14, 15, 16.5, 18) cm

1"
2.5 cm

2 (2, 2, 2¹/₂, 2¹/₂)"
5 (5, 5, 6.5, 6.5) cm

SLEEVE

Wrist
7 (7¹/₂, 8¹/₂, 9, 9¹/₂)"
18 (19, 21.5, 23, 24) cm

11¹/₂ (13, 14¹/₂, 15¹/₂, 16¹/₂)"
29 (33, 37, 39.5, 42) cm

FRONT
&
BACK

11 (12, 13, 14, 15)"
28 (30.5, 33, 35.5, 38) cm
Shoulder

8¹/₂ (9¹/₂, 10¹/₂, 11¹/₂, 12)"
21.5 (24, 26.5, 29, 30.5) cm

24 (26, 28, 30, 32)"
61 (66, 71, 76, 81.5) cm

FRONT

Transfer sts from holder to needle. Work as for Back until Front measures 3 (3½, 4, 4, 4½) inches for Child, 5½ (6½, 7, 7, 7½) inches for Adult, having completed a purl row. On the following row, k18 (20, 21, 22, 24) sts for Child, 26 (29, 32, 35, 38) sts for Adult, and place these sts on a holder for Left Front shoulder; bind off 14 (14, 16, 16, 18) sts for Child, 18 (20, 22, 24, 26) sts for Adult; knit rem sts for Right Front shoulder. Decrease at neck edge on RS rows 5 times for Child, 6 times for Adult, as follows: knit 1, ssk, work to end of row. When decs are complete, work straight until armhole measures same as Back. Place sts on holder.

Transfer sts for Left Front shoulder from holder to needle and work to correspond to Right Front shoulder. Decreases are worked at neck edge by working across to last 3 sts, k2tog, k1.

JOIN SHOULDERS

Turn sweater ws out. With RS together, place sts for Back on a straight needle, and join shoulders using the Three Needle Bind Off method. Turn work RS out.

NECK

Using smaller dpn and MC, begin at right shoulder seam. Pick up and k24 (24, 26, 28, 28) bound off sts for Child, 30 (32, 34, 36, 38) bound off sts for Adult, for Back neck. Pick up and k10 (10, 10, 12, 12) sts for Child, 14 (14, 14, 14, 14) sts for Adult, for side neck. Pick up and k14 (14, 16, 16, 18) bound off sts for Child, 18 (20, 22, 24, 26)

5 (5½, 6, 6½, 7) inches for Child, 8½ (9½, 10, 10, 10½) inches for Adult, having completed a purl row. On the following row, k13 (15, 16, 17, 19) sts for Child, 20 (23, 26, 29, 32) sts for Adult, for shoulder; bind off

24 (24, 26, 28, 28) sts for Child, 30 (32, 34, 36, 38) sts for Adult; k13 (15, 16, 17, 19) sts for Child, 20 (23, 26, 29, 32) sts for Adult, for second shoulder. Place shoulder sts on holder.

bound off sts for Adult, at Front neck; pick up and k10 (10, 10, 12, 12) sts for Child, 14 (14, 14, 14, 14) sts for Adult, for side neck. Knit 1 round in Color A, 1 round in Color B. Using MC, work 2 rounds of k1, p1 rib for Child, 4 rounds k1, p1 rib for Adult; then knit 4 rounds for Child, 6 rounds for Adult. Bind off loosely.

SLEEVE

Beginning at underarm and using larger (Size 9) dpn, pick up and k22 (24, 26, 28, 30) sts for Child, 36 (40, 42, 42, 44) sts for Adult, to shoulder seam; pick up and knit the same number of sts from shoulder seam to underarm. There are now 44 (48, 52, 56, 60) sts for Child, 72 (80, 84, 84, 88) sts for Adult.

Work in St st for 1½ (2, 2, 2, 2) inches for Child, 1 (1, 1, 1, 1) inch for Adult, and then begin dec as follows:
Round 1: Work to last 3 sts, k2tog, k1.
Round 2: Knit 1, sl 1, k1, psso, work to end of round.

Child: Decrease every inch 4 (4, 7, 8, 6) times. Then dec every ½ inch 3 (3, 0, 0, 3)

time(s). There are 30 (34, 38, 40, 42) sts. Then work straight until sleeve measures 7 (7½, 9, 10, 10) inches, or 1 inch less than desired length. Decrease evenly in next round 2 (4, 4, 4, 4) times. Change to smaller needles. Knit 1 round Color A, 1 round Color B. Using MC, work 2 rounds k1, p1 ribbing. Then k4 rounds. Bind off loosely. Work second sleeve exactly the same.

Adult: Decrease every inch 15 (15, 16, 16, 16) times. Then dec every 0 (½, ½, ½, ½) inch 0 (3, 3, 3, 4) time(s). There are 42 (44, 46, 46, 48) sts. Work straight until sleeve measures 14 (15, 16, 16, 16½) inches, or 1½ inches less than desired length. Decrease evenly in next round 4 (4, 6, 6, 6) times. Change to smaller needles. Knit 1 round Color A, 1 round Color B. Using MC, work 4 rounds k1, p1 ribbing and 4 rounds St st. Bind off loosely. Work second sleeve exactly the same.

FINISHING

Weave in loose ends.

For washing instructions read "Caring for Handknits" on page xiv.

PUNTA EDGED CAP

(Pictured in Vincent's Gold Mountain Mohair on page 31)

The *puntas* (points) are inspired by the incredible knitting of the Andes. *Puntas* done as fine as 28 stitches per inch edge many a colorful hat. Boys as young as ten learn the necessary skills, and knit their own hats.

An easy pattern.

SIZES
Child: Infant (2–4, 6–8 yrs)
Adult: Small (Medium, Large)

FINISHED MEASUREMENTS
Circumference: Child: 17 (18, 19)"/43 (45.5, 48.5) cm; **Adult:** 20 (21, 22)"/51 (53.5, 56) cm

GAUGE
16 sts & 24 rows = 4" (10 cm) in St st

MATERIALS
Yarn: Mountain Mohair
Main color (MC): 1 2 oz skein
Colors A & B: 1 2 oz skein each
Needles: Size 7 (4.5 mm) 16" (40 cm) circular; Size 7 (4.5 mm) dpn, or sizes required to obtain gauge

---

CAST ON 119 (126, 133) sts for Child, 140 (147, 154) sts for Adult, with Color A, using circular needle. Join sts, making sure sts are not twisted on needle, k1 st, pm on needle. This is where each round begins. With MC k1 round.

Puntas
NB: Puntas begin with a multiple of 7 stitches. When the Puntas are completed, a multiple of 4 sts remains.

Using Color B, *Knit 4 sts. Slide the last 2 of the 4 sts back onto left needle; knit them together (1 dec made). Knit 1; pick up the second and third sts from right needle and slip them over the first st (1 double dec has been made). Knit 2 sts. This completes 1 *punta,* which now has 4 sts. Repeat from * to end of round. There are 68 (72, 76) sts for Child, 80 (84, 88) sts for Adult, on needle. Continue for 1¾ (2, 2½) inches for Child, 2¾ (3, 3¼) inches for Adult.

Turn the work so that WS faces you. Using MC, k1 round. (This will leave a tiny hole; close when weaving in loose ends.) Continue knitting in MC for 3¼ (3¾, 4½); 5 (5½, 6) inches, then begin dec for top of hat.

First Dec Round
Infant: *K7, k2tog, k6, k2tog, repeat from * to end of round.
Sizes 2–4: *K7, k2tog, repeat from * to end of round.
Sizes 6–8: *K8, k2tog, k7, k2tog, repeat from * to end of round.
Size Sm: *K8, k2tog, repeat from * to end of round.
Size Med: *Knit 9, k2tog, k8, k2tog, repeat from * to end of round.
Size Lg: *K9, k2tog, repeat from * to end of round.
All sizes: Knit 1 round.

Second Dec Round
Infant: *K6, k2tog, k5, k2tog, repeat from * to end of round.

Sizes 2–4: *K6, k2tog, repeat from * to end of round.
Sizes 6–8: *K7, k2tog, k6, k2tog, repeat from * to end of round.
Size Sm: *K7, k2tog, repeat from * to end of round.
Size Med: *K8, k2tog, k7, k2tog, repeat from * to end of round.
Size Lg: *K8, k2tog, repeat from * to end of round.
All sizes: Knit 1 round.

Continue to dec in this manner every other round. With each succeeding dec round there will be 1 less st before "k2tog." Change to dpn when necessary, and work until 8 sts remain. Change to Color A and k2tog all around. Knit 5 (5, 5) rounds for Child, 7 (8, 8) rounds for Adult on these 4 sts.

FINISHING
Break yarn, leaving enough to draw through sts and fasten off. Weave loose ends into WS. For washing instructions read "Caring for Handknits" on page xiv.

Candace's Eyelet Sweater, Moriah's Wildflower Sweater & Cable Cardigan

CANDACE'S EYELET SWEATER

(Pictured in Moss Mountain Mohair)

Designer Candace Brown turns the easy yarn over Quatrefoil Eyelet Pattern on its side in this delicately textured cardigan or pullover. Knit sideways in two pieces, each section begins at the Seed Stitch cuff of the sleeve and works toward the center. The cardigan is joined at the center back; the pullover is joined at the backs and fronts. Choose a simple V-neck or narrow collar worked in Seed Stitch.

An advanced pattern.

SIZES
Petite (Small, Medium, Large)

FINISHED MEASUREMENTS
Chest: 39 (44, 50, 55)"/99 (112, 127, 139.5) cm
Length to shoulder: Long version all sizes: 25"/63.5 cm
Short version all sizes: 21"/53.5 cm
Length of sleeve on all sizes: 16¾" (42.5 cm)

GAUGE
4 sts = 1" (2.5 cm) on larger needle; Rows 1–16 of Quatrefoil Eyelet Pattern is 2¾" (7 cm); for accuracy, check gauge by casting on 16 sts with larger needles and completing the 16 rows of Quarterfoil Eyelet Pattern.

MATERIALS
Yarn
Mountain Mohair, 2 oz. skeins: **Long version:** 9 (10, 11, 12). **Short version:** 7 (8, 9, 10).
Double Twist or 2-Ply Wool, 4 oz skeins:
   Long version: 6 (6, 7, 7). **Short version:** 4 (5, 6, 6).
Needles: Sizes 7 (4.5 mm) & 9 (5.5 mm) 29" or 36" (80 cm) circular, or size required to obtain gauge
Buttons: ½"/1.5 cm: 8 for Long version; 6 for Short version
Holders: 2 spare long circular needles

NB: This sweater is knit from side to side. The width is determined by rows per inch. Length is determined by the number of sts cast on after sleeves have been knit. Please work to achieve the correct gauge.

PATTERN STITCHES
Quatrefoil Eyelet, a multiple of 8 sts:
Row 1(WS) and all other WS rows: Purl.
Row 2: Knit.
Row 4: K3, *yo, ssk, k6, repeat from *; last repeat will end k3 instead of k6.

Row 6: K1, *k2tog, yo, k1, yo, ssk, k3, repeat from *; last repeat will end k2 instead of k3.
Row 8: Repeat Row 4.
Row 10: Knit.
Row 12: K7, *yo, ssk, k6, repeat from *; end k1.
Row 14: K5, *k2tog, yo, k1, yo, ssk, k3, repeat from *; end k3.
Row 16: Repeat Row 12.

Seed Stitch on even number of sts:
Row 1: K1, p1, repeat to end of row.
Row 2: P1, k1, repeat to end of row.

RIGHT HALF OF SWEATER
Beginning at cuff and using Size 7 needle, cast on 40 sts. Do not join sts; work back and forth in Seed Stitch for 1-inch band.

Change to Size 9 needle and begin working Quatrefoil Eyelet. As the number of sts on the sleeve increases, work new Quatrefoils when there are 2 sts more than required for all 4 eyelets of the motif. When sleeves are completed and sts are added for Fronts and backs, the eyelets will match up if directions for inc and cast on sts have been followed exactly.

Keeping in patt, inc 1 st each end of every fifth row 10 times; then inc 1 st each end of every fourth row 9 times. There are now 78 sts. End with Row 8 of pattern. (Sleeve

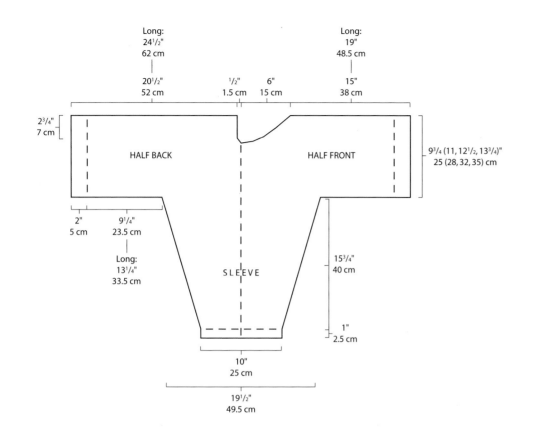

Long:
24½"
62 cm

20½"
52 cm

½"
1.5 cm

6"
15 cm

Long:
19"
48.5 cm

15"
38 cm

2¾"
7 cm

HALF BACK

HALF FRONT

9¾ (11, 12½, 13¾)"
25 (28, 32, 35) cm

2"
5 cm

9¼"
23.5 cm

Long:
13¼"
33.5 cm

SLEEVE

15¾"
40 cm

1"
2.5 cm

10"
25 cm

19½"
49.5 cm

should measure about 16¾ inches including the cuff after working 5½ repeats of the pattern.) Work Row 9 and at the end of this row cast on 61 sts for Long version or 45 sts for Short version. Begin next row with 8 sts of Seed Stitch; knit the rem sts (Row 10 of Quatrefoil Eyelet) and cast on 61 sts for Long version, or 45 sts for Short version, at the end of this row. There are now 200 sts for the Long version, or 168 sts for the Short version. Next row, work 8 sts in Seed Stitch, then Row 11 of Quatrefoil Eyelet, and end with 8 sts in Seed Stitch. Then, between the 8 sts of Seed Stitch at beginning and end of each row, continue to work Quatrefoil

Eyelet for approximately 7 (8¼, 9½, 11) inches from cast on sts, ending after completing Row 16 (8, 16, 8) before shaping neck.

Begin Neck for Right Half of Sweater
Purl Row 1 (9, 1, 9) of Quatrefoil Eyelet Pattern, reading Neck-Shaping Chart from *left* to *right*. This is the first row of chart for neck shaping. On second row of chart, knit across 90 sts for Long, 74 sts for Short; bind off next 11 sts; knit rem 99 [83] sts for Back. Continue working in patt on both Front and Back sts. On third row of chart, work across Back sts, dec 1 st at Back neck as

shown on chart; attach second ball of yarn for Front and bind off first 4 sts as shown in chart. Continue working chart, binding off as indicated. At the end of Row 4 (12, 4, 12) there are 97 [81] sts on Back, and 86 [70] sts for Front. At the end of Row 15 (7, 15, 7) there are 97 [81] sts for Back, and 76 [60] sts for Front.

Pullover: Place all sts on spare circular needle.

Cardigan: Place Back sts on spare circular needle. On sts for Front, continue by working 1 more row.

Front Band
Work in Seed Stitch. Change to smaller needles and work 2 rows. In the following row, begin buttonholes:

Long version: Work 2 sts, *bind off next 2 sts, work 8 sts, repeat from * until 4 sts remain; bind off next 2 sts and work last 2 sts.

Short version: Work 1 st, *bind off 2 sts, work 9 sts, repeat from * until 4 sts remain; bind off next 2 sts and work last 2 sts.

Both versions: In next row, continuing in Seed Stitch, cast on 2 sts above each pair of bound off sts. Work 2 more rows. Bind off very loosely, or use larger needle to bind off.

LEFT HALF OF SWEATER
Make a second piece exactly the same as Right Half until shaping for neck. Use

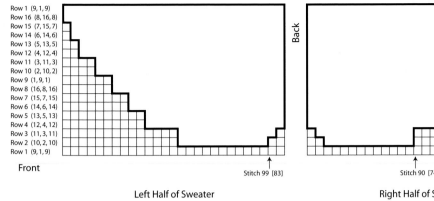

Row 1 (9, 1, 9)
Row 16 (8, 16, 8)
Row 15 (7, 15, 7)
Row 14 (6, 14, 6)
Row 13 (5, 13, 5)
Row 12 (4, 12, 4)
Row 11 (3, 11, 3)
Row 10 (2, 10, 2)
Row 9 (1, 9, 1)
Row 8 (16, 8, 16)
Row 7 (15, 7, 15)
Row 6 (14, 6, 14)
Row 5 (13, 5, 13)
Row 4 (12, 4, 12)
Row 3 (11, 3, 11)
Row 2 (10, 2, 10)
Row 1 (9, 1, 9)

Front

Back

Stitch 99 [83]

Left Half of Sweater

Row 1 (9, 1, 9)
Row 16 (8, 16, 8)
Row 15 (7, 15, 7)
Row 14 (6, 14, 6)
Row 13 (5, 13, 5)
Row 12 (4, 12, 4)
Row 11 (3, 11, 3)
Row 10 (2, 10, 2)
Row 9 (1, 9, 1)
Row 8 (16, 8, 16)
Row 7 (15, 7, 15)
Row 6 (14, 6, 14)
Row 5 (13, 5, 13)
Row 4 (12, 4, 12)
Row 3 (11, 3, 11)
Row 2 (10, 2, 10)
Row 1 (9, 1, 9)

Front

Stitch 90 [74]

Right Half of Sweater

Neck-Shaping Chart for Left Half of sweater as follows: Purl the first row of chart [Row 1 (9, 1, 9) of Eyelet Pattern], reading chart from *left* to *right*. On second row of chart, knit across 99 [83] Back sts; bind off the next 11 sts; knit rem 90 [74] sts for Front. On third row of chart, purl across Front sts, attach a second ball of yarn for Back sts, dec 1 st at Back neck edge, and purl rem sts. Continue working chart, binding off as indicated. At the end of Row 4 (12, 4, 12) there are 97 [81] sts for Back, 86 [70] sts for Front. At the end of Row 16 (8, 16, 8) there are 97 [81] sts for Back, 76 [60] sts for Front.

JOIN CENTER BACKS, BOTH VERSIONS

Place WS of work together, RS facing outward. *NB: Because the Back sections are mirror images of each other, the eyelets at center back are opposite each other, not offset.* Beginning at the neck edge, join, using a tapestry needle to work the Kitchener Stitch as follows:

Kitchener Stitch: *Pass yarn through first st of front needle as though to knit and sl st off needle. Pass yarn through second st on front needle as though to purl; leave st on needle and pull yarn firmly, just enough to form st the same size as those of the garment. Pass yarn through first st on back needle as though to purl; sl st off needle. Pass yarn through second st of back needle as though to knit; leave st on needle and pull yarn firmly.

Repeat from * until no more sts remain; place a small safety pin at end of this row to mark Center Back.

This type of joining makes a knit row, blending the two pieces together without a visible seam. Join Center Fronts of pullover in the same manner.

COLLAR FOR CARDIGAN

With RS facing, using Size 9 needle pick up and k96 sts between the two Front Bands (48 sts each side of safety pin). Continue in Seed Stitch until Collar measures 2¼ inches. Bind off loosely.

NECKBAND FOR PULLOVER

With RS facing, beginning at Center Front and, using larger needle, pick up and k52 sts along Right Front to Center Back Neck, and another 52 sts from Center Back along Left Front, ending at Center Front. Place a marker on needle; join sts. In the following round, k2tog working into the back of the sts. Continue in Seed Stitch until 2 sts remain before marker; k2tog, working into the front of the sts. Repeat this round, maintaining Seed Stitch, for ¾ inch. Bind off sts.

FINISHING

Sew underarm and side seams. Weave in loose ends. For cardigan, sew buttons on left Front Band to correspond with buttonholes.

For washing instructions read "Caring for Handknits" on page xiv.

MORIAH'S WILDFLOWER SWEATER

(Pictured in Silver Brown Green Mountain Green on page 36)

Spinnery friend Candace Brown needed a quick birthday present for her wildflower-loving teenage daughter, Moriah. Classic and cropped, this cardigan is distinguished by its all-over Wildflower Knot Pattern, and complemented by Seed Stitch border at the neck, wrist, and hem. Set-in sleeves and a jewel neckline grant a certain elegance to the finished garment.

An intermediate pattern.

SIZES
Small (Medium, Large)

FINISHED MEASUREMENTS
Chest: 38 (42, 46)"/96.5 (108.5, 117) cm
Length to underarm: 10¼ (11½, 12)"/26 (29.5, 30.5) cm

GAUGE
16 sts & 24 rows = 4" (10 cm) in Wildflower Knot Pattern

MATERIALS
Yarn
Mountain Mohair: 7 (8, 8) 2 oz skeins
Green Mountain Green: 8 (9, 10) 2 oz skeins
Yarn Over: 6 (6, 7) 4 oz skeins
Needles: Size 7 (4.5 mm) & 9 (5.5 mm) straight, or sizes required to obtain gauge
Stitch holders: 1 large, 2 small; 6 (6, 7) small safety pins.
Buttons: 7 (7, 8) 1"/(2.5 cm)

PATTERN STITCHES
Seed Stitch
With *odd* number of sts, all rows: *K1, p1, repeat from *, end with k1.

With *even* number of sts:
Row 1: *K1, p1, repeat from *.
Row 2: *P1, k1, repeat from *.

Wildflower Knot
Rows 1 & 3 (WS): Purl.
Row 2: Knit.
Row 4: K5, *p3tog and leave these sts on left needle; yo, purl same 3 sts tog again and transfer them to right needle, k5; repeat from *. (NB: *You will have the same number of sts when the row is finished as you had when you began.*)
Rows 5, 6, 7: Repeat Rows 1, 2, 3.

Row 8: K1, *p3tog, leave on left needle; yo, purl same 3 sts tog again, k5; repeat from *, ending with k1. (You still have the same number of sts!)

BACK
CAST ON 77 (85, 93) sts with smaller needles. Work Seed Stitch for 8 rows. Change to larger needles and begin Wildflower Knot. Work until entire piece measures 10¼ (11½, 12) inches or desired length to underarm. For all sizes, keeping in patt, bind off 4 sts at beginning of next 2 rows, 2 sts at beginning of following 2 rows. Then dec 1 st at beginning of next 4 rows. There are 61 (69, 77) sts on needle. Continue working in patt until armhole measures 9 (9, 10) inches. Bind off 6 (7, 8) sts at beginning of next 4 rows. Place rem 37 (41, 45) sts on large holder for neck Back.

LEFT FRONT
CAST ON 43 (47, 51) sts with smaller needle. Work Seed Stitch for 8 rows. Change to larger needles. Work first 8 sts in Seed Stitch for Front Band, and rem sts in Row 1 of Wildflower Knot. Continue in this manner. Row 4 of Wildflower Knot will begin with k3 (7, 3) instead of k5. Row 8 will begin with k7 (3, 7). Work until Left Front measures same as Back to underarm, having completed a WS row. On the following row, bind off 4 sts. Work the next row. Continue dec at armhole by binding off 2 sts on the following row and then dec 1 st every other row 2 times, leaving 35 (39, 43) sts. Work straight until armhole measures 5 (5, 6) inches, ending with a WS row. On the following row, place the 8 Front Band sts on a small stitch holder and work in patt across rem sts. Work 1 more row, and at the begin-

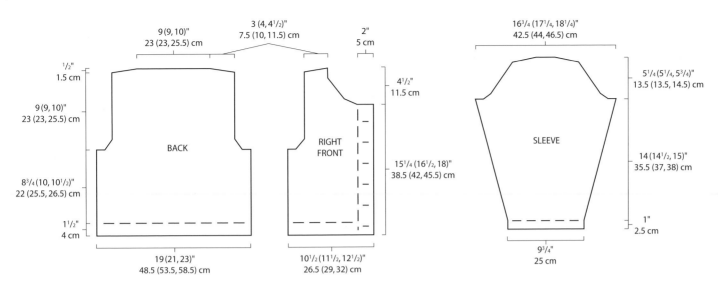

BACK

9 (9, 10)"
23 (23, 25.5) cm

3 (4, 4½)"
7.5 (10, 11.5) cm

2"
5 cm

½"
1.5 cm

9 (9, 10)"
23 (23, 25.5) cm

4½"
11.5 cm

8¾ (10, 10½)"
22 (25.5, 26.5) cm

RIGHT
FRONT

15¼ (16½, 18)"
38.5 (42, 45.5) cm

1½"
4 cm

19 (21, 23)"
48.5 (53.5, 58.5) cm

10½ (11½, 12½)"
26.5 (29, 32) cm

16¾ (17¼, 18¼)"
42.5 (44, 46.5) cm

SLEEVE

5¼ (5¼, 5¾)"
13.5 (13.5, 14.5) cm

14 (14½, 15)"
35.5 (37, 38) cm

1"
2.5 cm

9¾"
25 cm

Wildflower Knot pattern stitch

ning of next row bind off 4 (5, 6) sts. Continue by binding off 2 sts at neck edge 2 (2, 3) times; then dec 1 st at neck edge every other row 4 (5, 5) more times: 15 (17, 18) sts. Work until same length as Back, then bind off 7 (8, 9) sts on armhole edge. Work 1 row and then bind off rem 8 (9, 9) sts.

Place small safety pins in Front Band to indicate placement of buttons. The first button will be ¾ inch from bottom edge. Allow for the last button to be in the Neckband, which will be worked later.

RIGHT FRONT

CAST ON 43 (47, 51) sts with smaller needle. Work Seed Stitch for 3 rows. Continuing in Seed Stitch, make buttonhole in next row by working to last 5 sts, bind off next 2 sts, complete the row. On the following row, cast on 2 sts over bound off buttonhole sts. Work 3 more rows in Seed Stitch and change to larger needles. Work Row 1 of Wildflower Knot for 35 (39, 43) sts; keep

the rem 8 sts in Seed Stitch for Front Band. Continue in this manner, remembering to work buttonholes corresponding to placement of safety pins in Left Front. Row 4 of Wildflower Knot will end k3 (7, 3). Row 8 will end k7 (3, 7).

Work to same size as Left Front, reversing shaping for armhole and neck. Sew shoulder seams.

NECKBAND

With RS of work facing and smaller needles, work the 8 sts of the Right Front Band in Seed Stitch. Continuing in Seed Stitch, pick up 18 (20, 22) sts along neck edge, work the 37 (41, 45) sts from Back neck, pick up 18 (20, 22) sts along left neck edge, work the 8 sts of Left Front Band. There are 89 (97, 105) sts. Work Seed Stitch for 3 rows. Work the final buttonhole in the following 2 rows. Work 1 more row and then bind off.

SLEEVE

With smaller needles cast on 39 sts for all sizes and work Seed Stitch for 6 rows. Change to larger needles and begin Wildflower Knot. Row 4 will begin and end with k6. Keeping in patt, inc 1 st each end of row every ¾ inch 14 (15, 17) times, ending with 67 (69, 73) sts. Work even until entire piece measures 15 (15½, 16) inches or desired length to underarm. Begin to shape the sleeve cap by binding off 4 sts at the beginning of the next 2 rows, 2 sts at the beginning of the following 2 rows. Then dec 1 st each side every other row 11 (11, 13) times. Bind off 4 sts at the beginning of the next 6 rows. Bind off the rem 9 (11, 11) sts. Make a second sleeve to match.

FINISHING

Sew sleeves into armholes; sew side and underarm seams. Sew on buttons. Weave in all loose ends. For washing instructions read "Caring for Handknits" on page xiv.

CABLE CARDIGAN

(Pictured in White Double Twist Worsted Weight Wool on page 36)

An ideal introduction to cables. Handsome cables are worked front and back. Stitches are bound off at the armholes; sleeves are knit from the wrist up, and then are sewn into the straight armholes. Seed Stitch button bands and neck edge added last reflect the simple purl stitch pinstriping that frames the cable bands.

An intermediate pattern.

SIZES
Petite (Small, Medium, Large, X-Large)

FINISHED MEASUREMENTS
Chest: 36 (40, 44, 48, 52)"/91.5 (101.5, 112, 122, 132) cm
Length to shoulder: 22½ (24, 26½, 27½, 28)"/57 (61, 67.5, 70, 71) cm

GAUGE
18 sts & 24 rows = 4" (10 cm) in St st

MATERIALS
Yarn
Double Twist or 2-Ply Wool: 5 (6, 7, 7, 8) 4 oz skeins
Mountain Mohair: 9 (10, 11, 12, 13) 2 oz skeins
Green Mountain Green: 10 (12, 13, 14, 15) 2 oz skeins
Needles: Size 8 (5.0 mm) 29" or 36" (80 cm) circular, or size required to obtain gauge; 2 spare straight needles of any size for knitting shoulders together; cable needle (cn)
Stitch holders: 2 large, 2 small
Buttons: 7 (7, 8, 8, 8) ⅝"/2.0 cm

CABLE PATTERN (OVER 25 STS)
Rows 1 & 3: P7, k1, p9, k1, p7.
Row 2: P1, k2, p1, k3, p1, turn cable (transfer 3 sts to cn and hold in back of work, k1, k3 sts from cn, k1, transfer next st to cn and hold in front of work, k3, k1 from cn) p1, k3, p1, k2, p1.
Row 4: P1, k2, p1, k3, p1, k9, p1, k3, p1, k2, p1.

BODY
CAST ON 161 (179, 197, 215, 233) sts.
Work in Seed Stitch for 6 rows as follows:

Seed Stitch
Row 1 (RS): K1, p1 across row; end with k1.
Row 2 (WS): P2, *k1, p1, repeat from *, end with p1.

Then work Set Up Row for pattern as follows:

Set Up Row
K8 (10, 12, 14, 15) *p1, k2, p1, k3, p1, k3, m1, k1, m1, k3, p1, k3, p1, k2, p1*, k15 (22, 26, 30, 37), repeat from * to *, k23 (23, 29, 35, 37), repeat * to *, k15 (22, 26, 30, 37), repeat from * to *, k8 (10, 12, 14, 15). There are a total of 169 (187, 205, 223, 241) sts.

Continue by repeating the following 4 rows until entire piece measures approximately 14 (15, 17, 18, 18) inches or desired length to underarm, ending with Row 3.
Rows 1 & 3: P8 (10, 12, 14, 15), work Row 1 or 3 from Cable Pattern, p15 (22, 26, 30, 37), work Row 1 or 3 from Cable Pattern, p23 (23, 29, 35, 37), work Row 1 or 3 from Cable Pattern, p15 (22, 26, 30, 37), work Row 1 or 3 from Cable Pattern, p8 (10, 12, 14, 15).
Row 2: K8 (10, 12, 14, 15), work Row 2 from Cable Pattern, k15 (22, 26, 30, 37), work Row 2 from Cable Pattern, k23 (23, 29, 35, 37), work Row 2 from Cable Pattern, k15 (22, 26, 30, 37), work Row 2 from Cable Pattern, k8 (10, 12, 14, 15).
Row 4: K8 (10, 12, 14, 15), work Row 4 from Cable Pattern, k15 (22, 26, 30, 37), work Row 4 from Cable Pattern, k23 (23, 29, 35, 37), work Row 4 from Cable Pattern, k15 (22, 26, 30, 37), work Row 4 from Cable Pattern, k8 (10, 12, 14, 15).

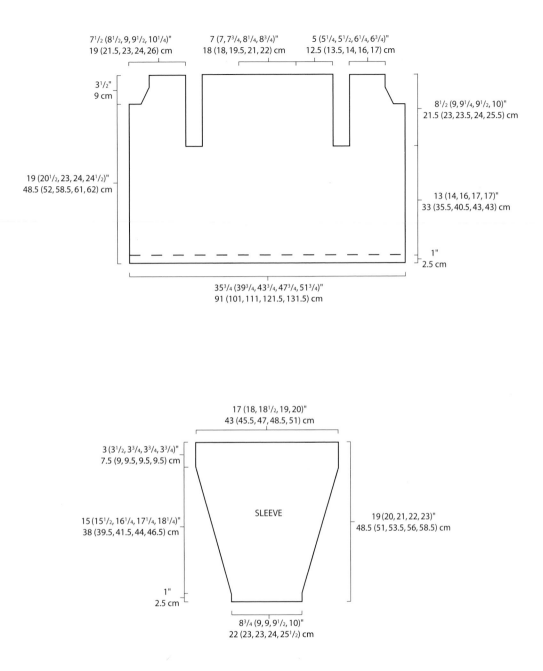

7½ (8½, 9, 9½, 10¼)"
19 (21.5, 23, 24, 26) cm

7 (7, 7¾, 8¼, 8¾)"
18 (18, 19.5, 21, 22) cm

5 (5¼, 5½, 6¼, 6¾)"
12.5 (13.5, 14, 16, 17) cm

3½"
9 cm

8½ (9, 9¼, 9½, 10)"
21.5 (23, 23.5, 24, 25.5) cm

19 (20½, 23, 24, 24½)"
48.5 (52, 58.5, 61, 62) cm

13 (14, 16, 17, 17)"
33 (35.5, 40.5, 43, 43) cm

1"
2.5 cm

35¾ (39¾, 43¾, 47¾, 51¾)"
91 (101, 111, 121.5, 131.5) cm

17 (18, 18½, 19, 20)"
43 (45.5, 47, 48.5, 51) cm

3 (3½, 3¾, 3¾, 3¾)"
7.5 (9, 9.5, 9.5, 9.5) cm

SLEEVE

15 (15½, 16¼, 17¼, 18¼)"
38 (39.5, 41.5, 44, 46.5) cm

19 (20, 21, 22, 23)"
48.5 (51, 53.5, 56, 58.5) cm

1"
2.5 cm

8¾ (9, 9, 9½, 10)"
22 (23, 23, 24, 25½) cm

DIVIDE FOR ARMHOLES

On Row 4, keeping in patt, work 36 (40, 42, 45, 48) sts and place them on a holder for Right Front; bind off 9 (12, 16, 18, 21) sts; work next 79 (83, 89, 97, 103) sts for Back; place rem 45 (52, 58, 63, 60) sts on a holder. Continue working Back in patt until armhole measures 8½ (9, 9¼, 9½, 10) inches, ending with Row 3 of pattern. On Row 4, work across 24 (26, 27, 30, 32) sts and place them on a holder; bind off 31 (31, 35, 37, 39) sts for neck; work across rem 24 (26, 27, 30, 32) sts and place them on a holder.

RIGHT FRONT

Transfer sts from holder onto needle; begin on WS row and work Row 1 of Cable Pattern. Continue to work in patt until armhole measures 5 (5½, 6, 6, 6½) inches. Beginning at neck edge, bind off 7 (9, 10, 10, 11) sts. Then dec at neck edge every other knit row 5 times as follows: Ssk, work to end of row. Continue on rem 24 (26, 27, 30, 32) sts until Front measures same as Back.

LEFT FRONT

Bind off 9 (12, 16, 18, 21) sts for underarm; work rem 36 (40, 42, 45, 48) sts using Row 4 of Cable Pattern. Continue on these sts, shaping to correspond to Right Front. The decs at neck edge will be on purl rows; purl the first 2 sts of the row together.

JOIN SHOULDERS

Join shoulders using the Three Needle Bind Off method as described in "Using the Patterns" on page xv.

FRONT BANDS

Left: Pick up and knit 3 sts for every 4 rows along Left Front, making sure to end with an odd number of sts. Work in Seed Stitch for 6 rows. (*k1, p1, repeat from * across, end k1.) Bind off.

Right: Work as for Left, placing 6 (6, 7, 7, 7) buttonholes in the second Seed Stitch row. Spacing should allow for the 7th (7, 8, 8, 8) buttonhole, which will be placed in Neckband. To make a buttonhole, bind off 1 st in Row 2. On next row, cast on 1 st above bound off st.

NECKBAND

With RS facing out, pick up and knit the following sts: 6 sts (all sizes) from Front Band, 6 (8, 9, 9, 10) bound off sts at Front neck, 12 sts (all sizes) at side neck, 31 (31, 35, 37, 39) bound off sts at back neck, 12 sts (all sizes) at side neck, 6 (8, 9, 9, 10) bound off sts at Front neck, 6 sts (all sizes) from Front Band for a total of 79 (83, 89, 91, 95) sts. Work 6 rows of Seed Stitch pattern. On the first Seed Stitch row, dec 1 st by knitting 2 tog at each of the inner corners. Work the 7th (7, 8, 8, 8) buttonhole directly above the other buttonholes in Right Front Band.

SLEEVES

CAST ON 39 (41, 41, 43, 45) sts and work 6 rows of Seed Stitch as for Front Bands. On the following row, k8 (9, 9, 10, 11) sts and then work between * and as in Set Up Row; k8 (9, 9, 10, 11) sts. There are now 41 (43, 43, 45, 47) sts. Begin the pattern as follows:

Rows 1 & 3: P8 (9, 9, 10, 11), work Row 1 or 3 from Cable Pattern, p8 (9, 9, 10, 11) sts.

Row 2: K8 (9, 9, 10, 11), work Row 2 from Cable Pattern, k8 (9, 9, 10, 11) sts.

Row 4: K8 (9, 9, 10, 11), work Row 4 from Cable Pattern, k8 (9, 9, 10, 11) sts.

Keeping in patt, inc 1 st each side of sleeve every fourth row 9 (10, 11, 11, 11) times; then inc every sixth row 9 (9, 9, 10, 11) times. There are now 77 (81, 83, 87, 91) sts. Work straight until sleeve is 19 (20, 21, 22, 23) inches long or desired length. Bind off all sts. Make a second sleeve to match.

FINISHING

Join top of sleeve to shoulder edge of arm-hole. Being careful to make square corner, sew about 1½ inches of upper sleeve edge to cast off sts at bottom of the armhole. Sew underarm seam. Sew on buttons. Weave in loose ends.

For washing instructions read "Caring for Handknits" on page xiv.

Norwegian Roses—This richly patterned cardigan is an open invitation to experiment with the entire Mountain Mohair rainbow of colors. The sweater's basic construction is a fine stage for any color combination you can imagine.

*Norwegian Roses
Cardigan*

Norwegian Roses Cardigan

(Pictured in Wintergreen, Ice Blue, Periwinkle, and Sky Blue Mountain Mohair on page 45)

Inspired by a design from Spinnery friend Nancy Oakes, this pattern invites several colorways in Mountain Mohair. The back and both sides of the front are worked as one piece, eliminating side seams. Because of the large number of stitches, this cardigan is made on a circular needle, working back and forth. The front bands and neck are four rows of single crochet; sleeve cuffs are turned under and sewn in place for double thickness. Destined to be become your "special occasion" winter jacket!

An intermediate pattern.

SIZES
Small (Medium, Large, X-Large)

FINISHED MEASUREMENTS
Chest: 40" (44, 48, 52)/101.5 (112, 122, 132) cm
Length to underarm: 16"/40.5 cm
Length to shoulder: 26"/66 cm
Length of sleeve: 18"/45.5 cm
NB: Length of body can be increased as much as 3 inches by adding 1 row in each Check Pattern, and by adding a row of solid color before and after each Check Pattern. The sleeves can be lengthened up to 2 inches in the same manner.

GAUGE
20 sts & 22 rows = 4" (10 cm) in 2-color pattern

MATERIALS
Yarn
Mountain Mohair, Double Twist or 2-Ply Wool (see colorways on page 47)
Needles: Sizes 6 (4.0 mm) & 7 (4.5 mm), circular 29" or 36" (80 cm); 1 pair Size 6 (4.0 mm) straight, or sizes required to obtain gauge
Crochet hook: Size E
Stitch holders: 3 small, 1 very large
Buttons: ½ to ¾"/1.5 to 2.0 cm: 10

BODY
CAST ON 202 (222, 242, 262) sts, using smaller circular needle and Color A (first listed color); work 5 rows Garter stitch (knit each row). Change to larger circular needle and proceed in St st. Work charts from *right* to *left* on knit rows, from *left* to *right* on purl rows. When it is necessary to change the number of sts for a chart, inc or dec evenly spaced throughout the row; *do not* inc or dec right at the beginning or end of a row. Work 2 rows St st Color A and then follow the charts on pages 48–49 as noted:

Checks

Hearts: On Row 2, dec 1 st for Sm & Lg; inc 3 sts for Med & XL: 201 (225, 241, 265) sts. On last row, inc 1 st for Sm & Lg; dec 3 sts for Med & XL: 202 (222, 242, 262) sts.

Checks

Leaves 1: On Row 2, dec 1 st for Sm & XL; inc 3 sts for Med, 1 st for Lg: 201 (225, 243, 261) sts. On last row, dec 4 sts for Med, 2 sts for Lg: 201 (221, 241, 261) sts.

Roses

Leaves 2: On Row 2, inc 4 sts for Med, 2 sts for Lg: 201 (225, 243, 261) sts. On last row, dec 1 st for Sm & XL; dec 3 sts for Med, 1 st for Lg: 202 (222, 242, 262) sts.

Roses

Leaves 1: On Row 2, inc 4 sts for Med, 2 sts for Lg: 201 (225, 243, 261) sts. On last row, inc 1 st for Sm & XL; dec 3 sts for Med, 1 st for Lg: 202 (222, 242, 262) sts.

Norwegian Roses Colorways

Colorway 1

Wintergreen	5 (6, 6, 7) 2 oz skeins
Ice Blue	3 (4, 4, 5) 2 oz skeins
Periwinkle	2 (2, 3, 3) 2 oz skeins
Sky Blue	1 (1, 1, 1) 2 oz skeins

Colorway 2

Glacier Lake	5 (6, 6, 7) 2 oz skeins
Periwinkle	3 (4, 4, 5) 2 oz skeins
Coral Bell	2 (2, 3, 3) 2 oz skeins
Day Lily	1 (1, 1, 1) 2 oz skeins

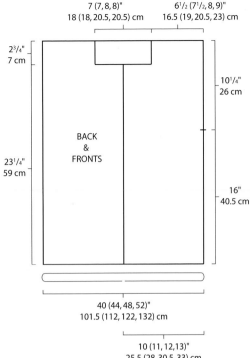

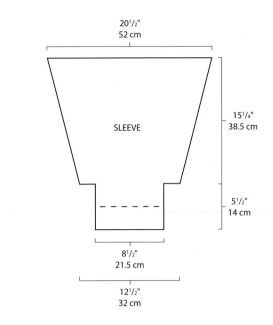

Checks

Vine: On Row 2, dec 1 st for Sm, Med & XL; inc 1 st for Lg: 201(221, 243, 261) sts. On last row, inc 1 st for Sm, Med & XL; dec 1 st for Lg: 202 (222, 242, 262) sts.

Checks

Right Front Yoke: Begin with a knit row. (If you have just completed a knit row, slide the sts to the other end of circular needle and attach Color A to work a knit row.) Using Color A, k50 (55, 60, 65) sts; place rem sts on large holder. Work 2 more rows Color A; then work:

Trellis & Hearts, Right Front Yoke: Work an additional 2 rows St st in Color A. On the following row, using Color A, bind off 16 (16, 18, 18) sts at Neck edge. (If the neck edge is at the end of the row, break yarn and reattach as needed.) There are 34 (39, 42, 47) sts. Then work:

Checks

Hearts, Right Front Yoke

Checks

Work 2 rows St st Color A and place sts on small holder.

Back Yoke: Using Color A, k102 (112, 122, 132) sts from holder, leaving 50 (55, 60, 65) sts on holder for Left Front Yoke. Work 2 more rows Color A, dec 1 st for Sm & Lg, and inc 1 st for Med & XL: 101 (113, 121, 133) sts. Then work the following:

Trellis, Back Yoke: Repeat pattern until Trellis is same length as for Right Front. Next, work 3 rows Color A, inc 1 st for Sm & Lg, and dec 1 st for Med & XL: 102 (112, 122, 132) sts.

Checks: Make the color sequence of these checks match the checks just below Trellis, Back Yoke.

Hearts, Back Yoke: On Row 2, dec 1 st for Sm, Lg & XL, and inc 1 st for Med: 101 (113, 121, 131) sts. On last row, inc 1 st for Sm, Lg & XL, and dec 1 st for Med: 102 (112, 122, 132) sts.

Checks

Work 2 rows Color A. Still using Color A, work across 34 (39, 42, 47) sts; place these sts on holder. Bind off 34 (34, 38, 38) sts;

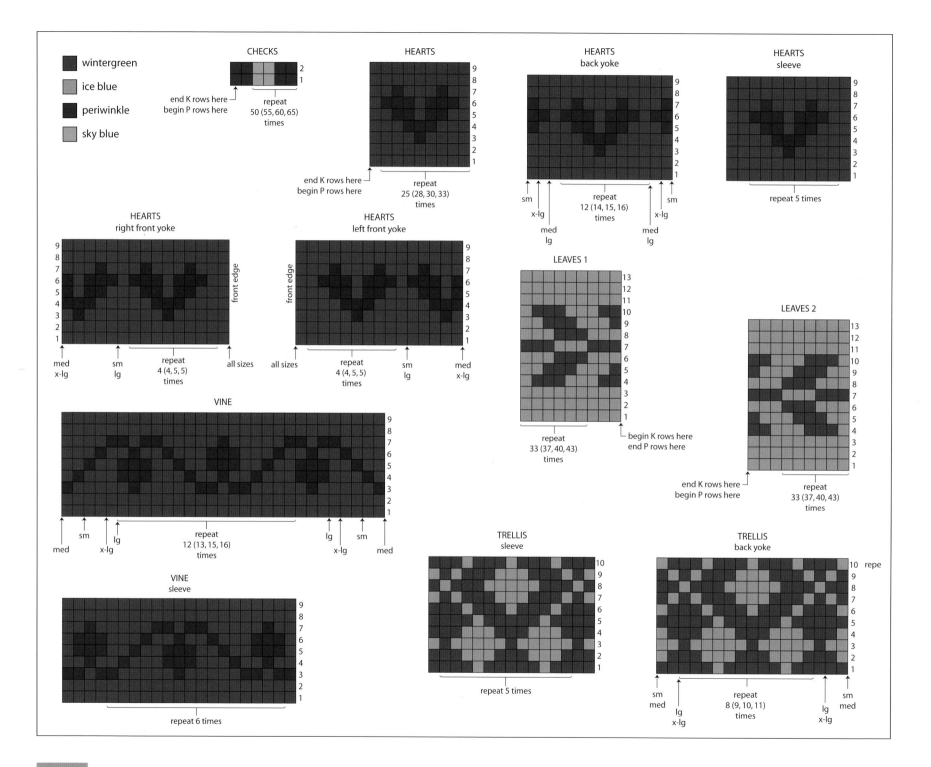

wintergreen
ice blue
periwinkle
sky blue

CHECKS

end K rows here
begin P rows here

repeat
50 (55, 60, 65)
times

2
1

HEARTS

9
8
7
6
5
4
3
2
1

end K rows here
begin P rows here

repeat
25 (28, 30, 33)
times

HEARTS
back yoke

9
8
7
6
5
4
3
2
1

sm
x-lg
med
lg

repeat
12 (14, 15, 16)
times

med
lg
x-lg
sm

HEARTS
sleeve

9
8
7
6
5
4
3
2
1

repeat 5 times

HEARTS
right front yoke

9
8
7
6
5
4
3
2
1

front edge

med
x-lg

sm
lg

repeat
4 (4, 5, 5)
times

all sizes

HEARTS
left front yoke

9
8
7
6
5
4
3
2
1

front edge

all sizes

repeat
4 (4, 5, 5)
times

sm
lg

med
x-lg

LEAVES 1

13
12
11
10
9
8
7
6
5
4
3
2
1

repeat
33 (37, 40, 43)
times

begin K rows here
end P rows here

LEAVES 2

13
12
11
10
9
8
7
6
5
4
3
2
1

end K rows here
begin P rows here

repeat
33 (37, 40, 43)
times

VINE

9
8
7
6
5
4
3
2
1

med
sm
x-lg
lg

repeat
12 (13, 15, 16)
times

lg
x-lg
sm
med

VINE
sleeve

9
8
7
6
5
4
3
2
1

repeat 6 times

TRELLIS
sleeve

10
9
8
7
6
5
4
3
2
1

repeat 5 times

TRELLIS
back yoke

10
9
8
7
6
5
4
3
2
1

repe

sm
med
lg
x-lg

repeat
8 (9, 10, 11)
times

lg
x-lg
sm
med

48

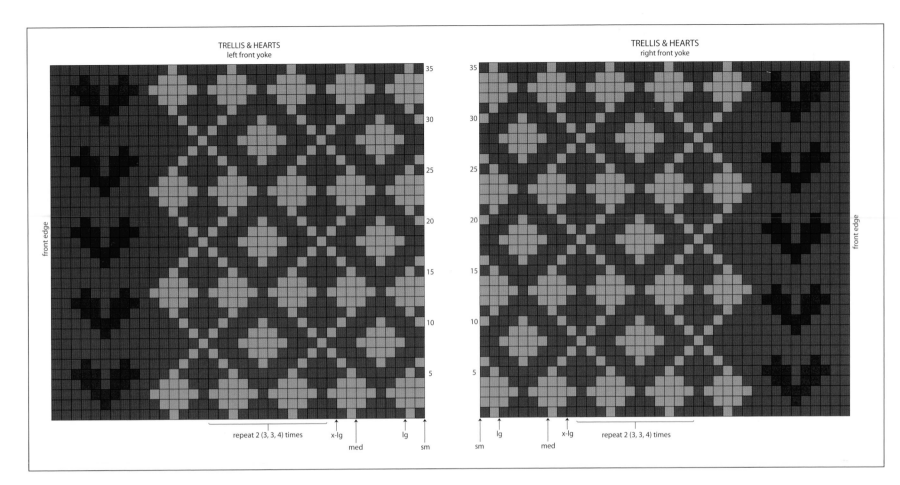

TRELLIS & HEARTS
left front yoke

TRELLIS & HEARTS
right front yoke

repeat 2 (3, 3, 4) times   x-lg   med   lg   sm

sm   lg   med   x-lg   repeat 2 (3, 3, 4) times

front edge

front edge

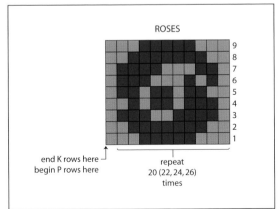

ROSES

9
8
7
6
5
4
3
2
1

end K rows here
begin P rows here

repeat
20 (22, 24, 26)
times

work across rem 34 (39, 42, 47) sts and place them on holder.

Left Front Yoke: Shape to correspond to Right Front Yoke. Reverse patterns as shown in charts for Left Front Yoke.

SLEEVES
CAST ON 42 sts, using Color A and Size 6 needle. Work 2¾ inches St st, ending with a knit row. Knit 1 row to make a Garter Stitch rib on RS; change to Size 7 needle and work 4 rows St st, beginning with a knit row.

Then work the following charts:

Checks

Hearts for sleeve: On Row 2, inc 1 st. On last row, dec 1 st.

Checks

Work 3 rows Color A, inc 1 st every other st in second row for a total of 63 sts Trellis, inc 1 st each end of every fourth row. (The chart indicates where the first row begins and ends.) Work added sts in Trellis Pattern; continue inc until there are 95 sts. Repeat the 10 pattern rows until entire sleeve measures approximately 15 inches, or 3 inches less than desired length, ending, if possible, with Row 5 or 8 of chart. Work 3 rows Color A, inc 3 sts in second row until there are 98 sts.

Checks

Vine, inc 1 st each end every 4 rows until there are 104 sts.

Checks: Make the color sequence of these checks correspond to the checks just below the Vine. This will mean the rows will begin and end differently than for the previous Checks.

Work 3 rows Color A. Bind off all sts.

JOIN SHOULDERS

Turn sweater WS out. To join shoulders, work a Three Needle Bind Off as described in "Using the Patterns" on page xv. Work with RS together. Then, turn work RS out. Sew sleeve seams and then sew sleeves into armholes.

FINISHING

Front Bands and neck: Work 2 rows of sc with a firm, even tension around Right Front, neck, and Left Front, working 3 sts in 1 where the neck meets the Front edge, and dec to shape the corners within the neck. The band needs to lie flat. On the Left Front, mark places for 10 buttons, evenly spaced. On the third row of sc, work buttonholes on Right Front, spaced as marked on Left Front. To form a buttonhole, chain 2 sts, skip over 2 sts, and then continue in sc. Work 1 more row of sc.

Sew on buttons and weave in all loose ends.

For washing instructions read "Caring for Handknits" on page xiv.

At right: Claire's Norwegian Roses colorway: Spice, Moss, and Rhubarb Mountain Mohair with Poppy Double Twist wool

At right: Lisa Lloyd's cabled tunic and pullover reflect the twists, turns, lush shadows, and winding brooks common along Vermont's quiet back roads. Woodland scenes and exuberant gardens inspired the colorways and texture of Melissa Lumley's steeked jacket for all ages.

Cable Weave Pullovers
& Green Mountain
Gardens Cardigan

CABLE WEAVE PULLOVER

(Pictured in Rhubarb and Balsam Mountain Mohair on page 51)

Designer Lisa Lloyd enjoys creating garments that are suited to all knitting abilities and won't go out of style. The Cable Weave Pullover features an easily memorized cable pattern that will challenge a beginner yet hold the interest of experienced knitters. Either version is well suited for either men or women and for comfortable wear.

An intermediate pattern.

FINISHED MEASUREMENTS

Chest: 34 (38, 42, 46, 50, 54)"/86.5 (96.5, 106.5, 117, 127, 137) cm

Version A (Scoop Neck shaping): Yoke depth of 16 (16½, 17, 18, 18½, 19½)"/40.5 (42, 43, 45.5, 47, 49.5) cm

Version B (Standard Crew Neck shaping): Yoke depth of 9 (9½, 10, 10½, 11, 12)"/23 (24, 25.5, 26.5, 28, 30.5) cm

GAUGE

16 sts & 24 rows = 4" (10 cm) in St st
19 sts & 31 rows = 4" (10 cm) in Cable Weave Pattern

MATERIALS

Yarn: Mountain Mohair: 8 (9, 10, 11, 12, 13) 2 oz skeins

Needles: Size 7 (4.5 mm) circular 24" or 29" (80 cm) and 16" (40 cm) circular or dpn; cable needle (cn)

Stitch holders: 3 medium

BACK

Both Versions: With longer circular needle, **CAST ON** 68 (76, 84, 92, 100, 108) sts for Back, pm on needle for side seam, cast on 68 (76, 84, 92, 100, 108) sts for Front, pm on needle for side seam, and join for a total of 136 (152, 168, 184, 200, 216) sts. Work Welt Pattern as follows:

Welt Pattern

Rounds 1 & 2: Purl.
Rounds 3 & 4: Knit.
Repeat Rounds 1–4 once more, then Rounds 1 and 2. Welt should measure approximately 1 inch.

Version A: Continue in St st, knitting each round, until lower Body measures 9 (9½, 10, 10, 10½, 10½) inches from beginning. Work Dividing Ridge as follows:

Version A: Scoop Neck

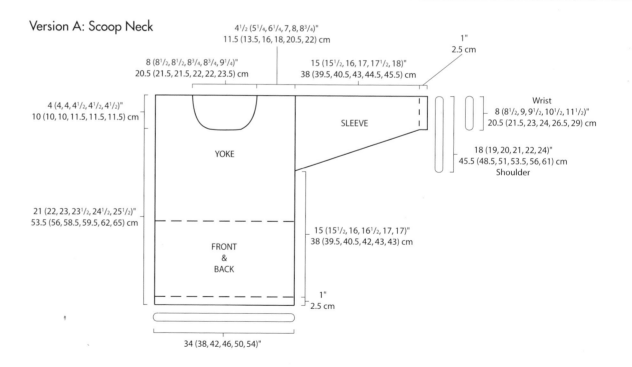

4½ (5¼, 6¼, 7, 8, 8¾)"
11.5 (13.5, 16, 18, 20.5, 22) cm

8 (8½, 8½, 8¾, 8¾, 9¼)"
20.5 (21.5, 21.5, 22, 22, 23.5) cm

15 (15½, 16, 17, 17½, 18)"
38 (39.5, 40.5, 43, 44.5, 45.5) cm

1"
2.5 cm

4 (4, 4, 4½, 4½, 4½)"
10 (10, 10, 11.5, 11.5, 11.5) cm

SLEEVE

Wrist
8 (8½, 9, 9½, 10½, 11½)"
20.5 (21.5, 23, 24, 26.5, 29) cm

YOKE

18 (19, 20, 21, 22, 24)"
45.5 (48.5, 51, 53.5, 56, 61) cm
Shoulder

21 (22, 23, 23½, 24½, 25½)"
53.5 (56, 58.5, 59.5, 62, 65) cm

15 (15½, 16, 16½, 17, 17)"
38 (39.5, 40.5, 42, 43, 43) cm

FRONT & BACK

1"
2.5 cm

34 (38, 42, 46, 50, 54)"

CABLE WEAVE PATTERN

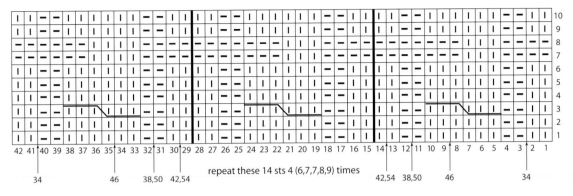

repeat these 14 sts 4 (6,7,7,8,9) times

34   46   38,50 42,54   42,54 38,50   46   34

KEY TO CHART

| | | | | | | | | | | | | sl next 3 sts to cn, hold in front, k3, k3 from cn

| I | K on right side rows, P on wrong side

| − | P on right side rows, K on wrong side

Begin and end chart as indicated for your size.
Each row of the chart is worked across back and repeated for front.

Version B: Crew Neck

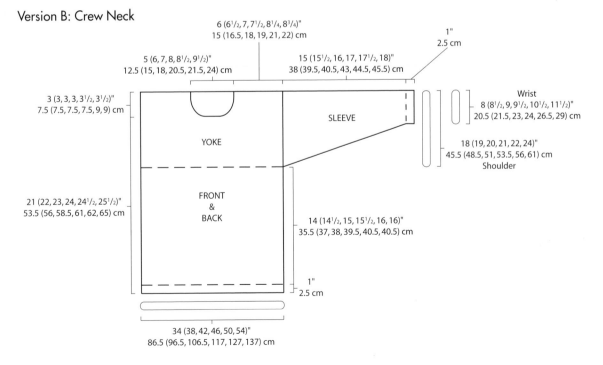

6 (6½, 7, 7½, 8¼, 8¾)"
15 (16.5, 18, 19, 21, 22) cm

1"
2.5 cm

5 (6, 7, 8, 8½, 9½)"
12.5 (15, 18, 20.5, 21.5, 24) cm

15 (15½, 16, 17, 17½, 18)"
38 (39.5, 40.5, 43, 44.5, 45.5) cm

Wrist
8 (8½, 9, 9½, 10½, 11½)"
20.5 (21.5, 23, 24, 26.5, 29) cm

3 (3, 3, 3, 3½, 3½)"
7.5 (7.5, 7.5, 7.5, 9, 9) cm

SLEEVE

YOKE

18 (19, 20, 21, 22, 24)"
45.5 (48.5, 51, 53.5, 56, 61) cm
Shoulder

21 (22, 23, 24, 24½, 25½)"
53.5 (56, 58.5, 61, 62, 65) cm

FRONT
&
BACK

14 (14½, 15, 15½, 16, 16)"
35.5 (37, 38, 39.5, 40.5, 40.5) cm

1"
2.5 cm

1"
2.5 cm

34 (38, 42, 46, 50, 54)"
86.5 (96.5, 106.5, 117, 127, 137) cm

Dividing Ridge
Round 1 & 2: Purl.
Round 3: Knit.
Round 4: Knit, increasing 24 (28, 32, 36, 36, 40) sts evenly across round. There are 160 (180, 200, 220, 236, 256) sts. Begin Cable Weave Pattern chart as indicated for your size. *NB: Be sure to knit the sts on Row 3 where there is not a complete cable at the side edges.*

Continue until Body measures 16 (16½, 17, 17½, 18, 18) inches from beginning.

Version B: Continue in St st until Body measures 15 (15½, 16, 16½, 17, 17) inches from beginning.

BACK: DIVIDE FOR ARMHOLES
Work back and forth.

Version A: Work 80 (90, 100, 110, 118, 128) sts in established patt for Back, place next 80 (90, 100, 110, 118, 128) sts for Front on length of contrast yarn. (Make note of last row of chart worked.) Continue working chart until Back measures 9 (9½, 10, 10½, 11, 12) inches from start of armhole. Place these sts on a holder.

Version B: Work Dividing Ridge as follows:

Dividing Ridge
Row 1: P68 (76, 84, 92, 100, 108) sts; place next 68 (76, 84, 92, 100, 108) sts for Front on length of contrast yarn.
Row 2 & 3: Knit.
Row 4: Purl, inc 12 (14, 16, 18, 18, 20) sts

evenly across row for a total of 80 (90, 100, 110, 118, 128) sts.

Begin Cable Weave Pattern chart as indicated for your size. *NB: Be sure to knit the sts on Row 3 where there is not a complete cable at the side and neck edges.*

Continue working patt until Back measures 9 (9½, 10, 10½, 11, 12) inches from start of armhole. Place these sts on a holder.

FRONT

Version A: Place Front sts on needle, and with RS facing, work as for Back until Front measures 5 (5½, 6, 6, 6½, 7½) inches from start of armhole. Begin to shape neck by working across 30 (35, 40, 44, 48, 53) sts; place center 20 (20, 20, 22, 22, 22) sts on a holder. Attach a second ball of yarn and work across rem sts. Working both sides at once, dec at neck edges 1 st every other row 9 (10, 10, 10, 10, 11) times. There are 21 (25, 30, 34, 38, 42) sts. Work even in patt until Front armhole measures the same as Back.

Version B: Place Front sts on needle, and with RS facing, work as for Back until Front measures 6 (6½, 7, 7½, 7½, 8½) inches from start of armhole.

Begin to shape neck by working across 30 (35, 40, 45, 49, 53) sts; place center 20 (20, 20, 20, 20, 22) sts on a holder. Attach a second ball of yarn and work across rem sts. Working both sides at once, dec at neck edges 1 st every other row 6 (6, 7, 7, 8, 8) times: 24 (29, 33, 38, 41, 45) sts remain.

Work even in patt until Front armhole measures the same as Back.

JOIN SHOULDERS

Both versions: Join first shoulder, working a Three Needle Bind Off as described in "Using the Patterns" on page xv. Then bind off the back neck sts, and join the second shoulder as the first.

NECK FINISHING

Version A: Beginning at right shoulder and with smaller circular needle or dpn, pick up and k34 (34, 34, 36, 36, 40) sts across Back neck; 12 (14, 14, 14, 14, 15) sts along left side neck; 20 (20, 20, 22, 22, 22) sts across center Front neck; 12 (14, 14, 14, 14, 15) sts along right side neck, for a total of 78 (82, 82, 86, 86, 92) sts around neck edge. Work Welt Pattern as follows:

Welt Pattern
Rounds 1 & 2: Purl, dec 2 sts evenly spaced in center Front and 2 sts in Back on Round 2.
Rounds 3 & 4: Knit.
Work Round 1 once more and bind off loosely in purl.

Version B: Beginning at right shoulder with smaller circular needle or dpn, pick up 32 (32, 34, 34, 36, 38) sts across Back neck; 12 (12, 12, 12, 14, 14) sts along left side neck; 20 (20, 20, 20, 20, 22) sts across center Front neck; 12 (12, 12, 12, 14, 14) sts along right side neck, for a total of 68 (70, 70, 72, 78, 82) sts around the neck edge. Work Welt Pattern as for Version A, without dec in Round 2.

SLEEVES

Both versions: With 24" circular needle, pick up 72 (76, 80, 84, 88, 96) sts evenly around armhole, ending at underarm. Place marker, join. Working in St st, dec 1 st on each side of marker every fourth round 16 (21, 20, 21, 15, 23) times, then every fifth round 4 (0, 2, 2, 8, 2) time(s). There are 32 (34, 36, 38, 42, 46) sts. Work even until sleeve measures 15 (15½, 16, 17, 17½, 18) inches in length. Work Welt Pattern as follows:

Welt Pattern
Rounds 1 & 2: Purl.
Rounds 3 & 4: Knit.
Repeat these 4 rounds once more and then Round 1 once. Bind off purlwise.

FINISHING
Weave in yarn ends.

For washing instructions read "Caring for Handknits" on page xiv.

Energized Vest

ENERGIZED VEST

(Pictured in Gray and White Energized Wool Singles on page 55)

Kathryn Alexander's cropped vest incorporates six rectangles in three simple patterns: Two patterns are worked in Stockinette Stitch, and the third is a knit four, purl four rib. The energized yarns give these stitches a distinctive texture. The placement of the pattern pieces is the same, but opposing, front and back. The Ribbed Block Pattern has no shaping; the remaining pieces are shaped for armholes and neckline.

An intermediate pattern.

FINISHED MEASUREMENTS
Chest: 48"/122 cm
Length: 21¾"/55 cm

FINISHED (MIGRATED STITCHES) GAUGES
4x4 Rib Blocks: 32 sts & 33 rows = 4" (10 cm) using midsized needle
Horizontal Stripes: 24 sts & 39 rows = 4" (10 cm) using midsized needle
Vertical Stripes: 30 sts & 29 rows = 4" (10 cm) using midsized needle
NB: It is important to work and finish gauge swatches for each pattern stitch.

MATERIALS
Yarn
Energized Wool Singles: 2 cones: 1 cone Gray-Z & 1 cone White-S, or 1 cone White-Z & 1 cone Gray-S
Needles: Sizes 2 (2.75 mm), 4 (3.5 mm) & 5 (3.75 mm) circular needles or size necessary to obtain gauge
Crochet hook: Size E (3.5 mm)
Stitch holders: 4 circular needles

A GUIDE TO WORKING WITH ENERGIZED WOOL SINGLES

What are Energized Singles? Energized Singles, S and Z twist, are yarns that have not been "steamed" or finished after being spun and wound onto a cone. The yarn on the cone is under tension, and this, along with time on the cone, puts the energy created during the spinning process into an at-rest state. Energy is present, but not visible. Z yarn is spun clockwise and S yarn is spun counter-clockwise. Cloth knit with energized Z yarn will slant to the right like the center of the letter Z. Cloth made with energized S yarn will slant to the left like the center of the letter S.

Yarn handling. Keep the yarn on the cones, thus maintaining the yarn's energy in an at-rest state. Energy in the yarn will yield to moisture at any level once off the cone. The yarn will become kinkier when it passes through your knitting hands because the heat and moisture will activate some of the yarn's energy. Resist the urge to stand cones upright and unload from the top of the cone. This would add (or subtract) energy from the yarn. Rather, pull the yarn from the side of the cone. An easy way to do this is to allow the cone to rotate on a straight knitting needle suspended from holes pierced in the side of a shoe box. Placing one shoe box with its suspended cone of yarn on your right and the other shoe box on your left will prevent the yarns from tangling as you knit.

Knitting with S & Z twist yarns: Typically, knitters throw or pick the yarn around the needle in a counterclockwise direction for both knitting and purling. Wrapping the Z yarn counterclockwise will *add* energy to the yarn, making it kinkier, while wrapping the S yarn in the same direction will *remove* energy, making the yarn less active. In order to maintain the same energy level in *both* yarns, simply wrap the S yarn clockwise around the needle. Since the resulting stitch will be twisted on the needle, work into the back of this S stitch with whichever yarn (S or Z) you are using on the following row. Working in this manner (i.e., wrapping Z counterclockwise and S clockwise) ensures an even stitch tilt across the cloth's surface.

Vertical stripes

Horizontal stripes

4 x 4 rib blocks

Rows 2, 4 & 6: *K4 gray, p4 white; repeat from * across row.

Rows 3 & 5: *K4 white, p4 gray; repeat from * across row.

Row 7: *K4 gray, k4 white; repeat from * across row.

Rows 8, 10 & 12: *K4 white, p4 gray; repeat from * across row.

Rows 9 & 11: *K4 gray, p4 white; repeat from * across row.

Horizontal Stripes (6-row repeat)

NB: This fabric will seem very loose before finishing.

Rows 1–3: Work St st, using white. Slide work down to opposite end of needle. Pick up gray yarn.

Rows 4–6: Work St st, using gray.

Vertical Stripes (2 sts, 2 rows)

NB: Always keep S yarn on top, working Z yarn from under S.

Row 1: *K1 white, k1 gray; repeat from * across row.

Row 2: *P1 gray, p1 white; repeat from * across row.

PATTERN
Right Back (Vertical Stripe)
Using midsized needle and gray, **CAST ON** 80 sts. Work 1x1 Vertical Stripe Pattern for 86 rows, ending with WS row.

Shape Armhole: Bind off 5 sts in patt every

Swatching & finishing: Do take the time to knit the test swatches to familiarize yourself with the patterns and the yarn. For an accurate gauge reading, measure the sample after it is "finished" or washed. To finish the swatch, leave it on the needle, then handwash and rinse it in hot water with a small amount of soap and slight agitation. This removes the spinning oil and awakens the yarn's energy. Since the energy has to go somewhere, the stitches will migrate or tilt to the left or right, creating the surface patterns and making the piece wider or longer side to side. Measure your swatch after the fabric is completely dry.

PROVISIONAL CROCHET CAST ON
This optional but recommended cast on is useful when you wish to have loops available at the bottom of the fabric with which to work an edge. Using waste yarn about the same weight as your project yarn and a crochet hook a few sizes larger than the designated knitting needles, loosely crochet a chain with at least as many stitches as the pattern indicates. With your knitting needles and project yarn, pick up the designated number of cast on stitches in the bumps at the back of the crochet chain. In order to work down from the cast on stitches, simply "unzip" the crochet chain from the knotted end and put the loose loops onto your knitting needle. Binding off the loops gives the fabric identical top and bottom edges.

PATTERN STITCHES
4x4 Rib Blocks (8 sts & 12 rows = 2 rows of blocks)

NB: Carry floats loosely across Back. Cross the yarns after the first 4 sts of each row to avoid making a hole between the blocks. Always keep S yarn on top, working Z yarn from under S. This will prevent the yarns from twisting around each other and will make working the clockwise wrap of the S yarn more efficient.

Row 1 (RS): *K4 white, k4 gray; repeat from * across row.

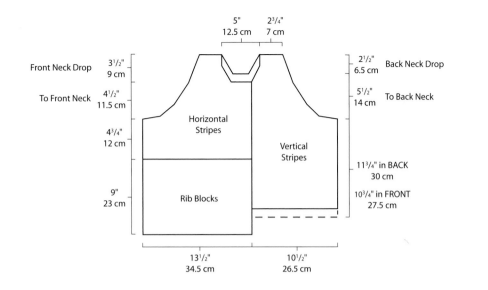

Front Neck Drop — 3½" / 9 cm
To Front Neck — 4½" / 11.5 cm
4¾" / 12 cm
9" / 23 cm

5" / 12.5 cm
2¾" / 7 cm

Horizontal Stripes

Vertical Stripes

Rib Blocks

2½" / 6.5 cm — Back Neck Drop
5½" / 14 cm — To Back Neck
11¾" in BACK / 30 cm
10¾" in FRONT / 27.5 cm

13½" / 34.5 cm
10½" / 26.5 cm

other row 5 times: 55 sts. Next RS row: *Ssk, work to end*. Rep between *s every RS row 21 times more. *At the same time,* when 41 sts rem, shape Right Back Neck. Next WS row: Purl 2 tog, work to end. Cont to dec at beg of WS rows 8 times more: 24 sts. Using gray, *k1, k2tog; rep from * across. Put 16 sts on holder. Bottom edge: Undo crochet chain of Provisional Cast On and put open sts onto smaller needle. Beginning with WS facing and using gray, k3 rows. Bind off in knit. Finish fabric (see page 56).

Left Front (Vertical Stripe)

Work as for Right Back for 78 rows. Shape armhole as for Right Back. *At the same time,* when 45 sts rem, shape Left Front neck as for Right Back neck. Work neck edge even until 24 sts rem. Using gray, *k1, k2tog; rep from * across. Put 16 sts on holder. Work bottom edge as for Right Back. Finish fabric.

Right Front (Horizontal Stripe)

Using Size 4 needle and white, provisionally **CAST ON** 80 sts. Work Horizontal Stripe Pattern until there are 13 3-row stripes. Work Row 4 of pattern.

Shape armhole:
Bind off 5 sts purlwise at beg of next 2 WS rows, then 3 sts, then 2 sts: 65 sts. (Hint: Use crochet hook to work idle yarn along bound off edge.) Decrease at armhole edge (either p2tog or k2tog, depending on which side is facing) every other row 5 times, then every 3 rows 20 times. *At the same time,* when 50 sts rem, shape Right Front neck: Work across next row, putting first 18 sts at neck edge on holder after having worked them: 32 sts. Dec at neck edge every 3 rows 6 times (either ssp or ssk). Work neck edge even until 16 sts rem. Work 3 rows even. Put on holder. Bottom edge: Undo crochet chain of Provisional Cast On and put open sts onto

midsized needle. Beginning with WS facing and using white, k5 rows. Bind off very loosely in knit. Finish fabric.

Left Back (Horizontal Stripe)

Work as for Right Front until 46 sts rem. Shape Left Back neck: Work same as for Right Front neck. Work neck edge even until 16 sts rem. Work 3 rows even. Put on holder. Work bottom edge as for Right Front. Finish fabric.

Rib Block Rectangle (make 2): Using mid-sized needle and white, provisionally **CAST ON** 72 sts. Begin 4x4 Rib Block Pattern. Work 19 rows of blocks. *Do not break yarn.* Place sts on extra needle and finish the piece. The dry, migrated fabric should be as long as the Horizontal Stripe piece is wide. If the piece is too short or too long, continue knitting or rip out as necessary. Bind off loosely in knit. Undo crochet chain of Provisional Cast On and put open sts onto needle used for main fabric. Bind off loosely in knit.

ASSEMBLY AND FINISHING

Right Front & Left Back: Pin the knit side edge of Rib Block Rectangle to Garter stitch bottom of Right Front. The top set of blocks should overlap Garter stitch edge. Using white, tack down top points in front, then sew down Garter stitch edge from back of fabric. Repeat for Back.

Front Seam: Using midsized needle and white, with RS facing, pick up 86 sts along center edge of Left Front; pick up 100 sts along Right Front (50 along Horizontal

Stripe edge, 50 along Rib Block bottom edge). With RS facing out and beginning at neck edge, work Three Needle Bind Off (ridge is to the outside). Bind off remaining sts along Rib Blocks in knit.

Back seam: Work as for Front, but pick up 96 sts along Right Back and 106 sts along Left Back (56 + 50).

Shoulder seams: With WS facing out, using midsized needle and gray, work Three Needle Bind Off (ridge is to the inside).

ARMHOLE EDGE

Using midsized needle and gray, with WS facing, pick up 129 sts. Work 1x1 Vertical Stripe Pattern for 6 rows, then change to larger (Size 5) needle and work 7 rows. Bind off very loosely in pattern (go up one more needle size if necessary). Turn the edge to the front. Tack down the bound off edge invisibly with the white tail by going down through the white stitch on the RS and back up through the gray on the back. Using white, overcast underarm seam after the garment side seams are finished.

Left side seam: Using midsized needle and white, pick up 62 sts along side edge of Left Front and 73 (23 + 50) sts along side edge of Left Front. With RS facing out and beginning at armhole, work Three Needle Bind Off; bind off rem sts knitwise.

Right Side Seam: Pick up 73 (23 + 50) sts along Right Front and 67 sts along Right Back. Work as for left side seam.

COLLAR

Using larger needle and gray, with RS facing, slide 18 sts from Front neck stitch holder onto needle, pick up 42 sts along neck to Back neck stitch holder, knit 18 sts from holder, pick up 42 sts along neck: 120 sts. Work in Rib Block Pattern for 12 rows; change to midsized needle and work 6 more rows. Using gray, bind off loosely in rib, going up a needle size if necessary.

FINISHING

Finish completed vest and block to size. Use pins to make points of Rib Block Pattern at hem and collar line. Weave in loose ends.

For washing instructions read "Caring for Handknits" on page xiv.

*Putney Aran
Tunic*

Putney Aran Tunic

(Pictured in Luminosity Sylvan Spirit and Storm Cotton Comfort)

Designer Lisa Lloyd pairs classic cable stitch patterns with two contemporary neck and hem styling choices. The cable pattern is carried from cuff to neckline with saddle sleeve styling. The "skirt" option makes this otherwise casual unisex design a bit more high fashion, depending on yarn choice. Both yarns offer lightweight, yet warm comfort. The multiple cable motifs and saddle sleeve construction will interest both beginning and experienced knitters.

An intermediate pattern.

FINISHED MEASUREMENTS
Chest: 37 (41, 45, 50, 54)"/94 (104, 114.5, 127, 137) cm
Version A length (with skirt): 27 (28, 29, 30, 31)"/68.5 (71, 73.5, 76, 78.5) cm
Version B length (without skirt): 27¾ (27¾, 27¾, 30¾, 30¾)"/70.5 (70.5, 70.5, 78, 78) cm
Sleeve length to underarm (both versions): Women's: 16¼ (15½, 17½, 17¼, 18¾)" 41.5 (39.5, 44.5, 44, 47.5) cm. **Men's:** 19¼ (18½, 20¼, 20½, 21¾)"/49 (47, 51.5, 52, 55) cm.

GAUGE
24 sts & 32 rows = 4" (10 cm) over chart pattern on larger needle
22 sts & 32 rows = 4" (10 cm) in St st/Reverse stitch on larger needle
NB: When working correct gauge of Body Charts A & C, each repeat of the 24 rows will measure 3"/7.5 cm.

MATERIALS
Yarn: Cotton Comfort or Sylvan Spirit 8: (9, 10, 11, 12) 2 oz skeins
Needles: Size 3 (3.25 mm) straight & 16" (40 cm) circular; Size 5 (3.75 mm) straight, or sizes required to obtain gauge; 1 spare needle
Stitch holder: 1 medium

VERSION A: BACK
With smaller needle, **CAST ON** 110 (120, 132, 144, 156) sts. Work in Garter Stitch (knit each row) for 8 rows (4 ridges). Begin Skirt Chart as follows:

Skirt Chart
Knit 6 (6, 5, 6, 5) sts, p0 (5, 0, 5, 0) st(s), work Skirt Repeats as indicated, end p0 (5, 0, 5, 0) sts, k6 (6, 5, 6, 5) sts. Continue until piece measures 5¼ (6¼, 7¼, 8¼, 9¼) inches from beginning, ending with Row 4. Work Garter Stitch across all sts for 8 rows (4 ridges).

Change to larger straight needle and work 4 rows in St st, inc 1 st each end of last row, ending 112 (122, 134, 146, 158) sts. Begin Body pattern as follows: P8 (13, 19, 25, 31) sts, work 24 sts Chart A, work Chart B over next 48 sts, work Chart C over next 24 sts, end p8 (13, 19, 25, 31) sts. Continue until piece measures 18 (18½, 18½, 19, 19) inches from beginning. Bind off 7 (11, 11, 11, 11) sts at beginning of next 2 rows for underarm. Continue working as established, until 6 repeats of Body Charts A & C are complete. Bind off all sts. There are 98 (100, 112, 124, 136) sts.

VERSION A: FRONT
Work as for Back, including underarm shaping, until piece measures ½ (½, ½, 1, 1) inch less than Back.

Begin neck shaping: Work across 34 (34, 39, 43, 48) sts of shoulder; place next 30 (32, 34, 38, 40) sts for Front neck on holder; join second ball of yarn and dec 1 st at neck edges, every other row 2 (2, 2, 4, 4) times. Work even until Front measures same length as Back. Bind off 32 (32, 37, 39, 44) sts on each shoulder.

Putney Aran Tunics—*Lisa Lloyd's Putney Aran is a classic example of how yarn choice reveals a pattern's versatility. Sylvan Spirit grants a cool elegance to the tunic version; Cotton Comfort lends an air of "everyday" casual to the unisex crewneck.*

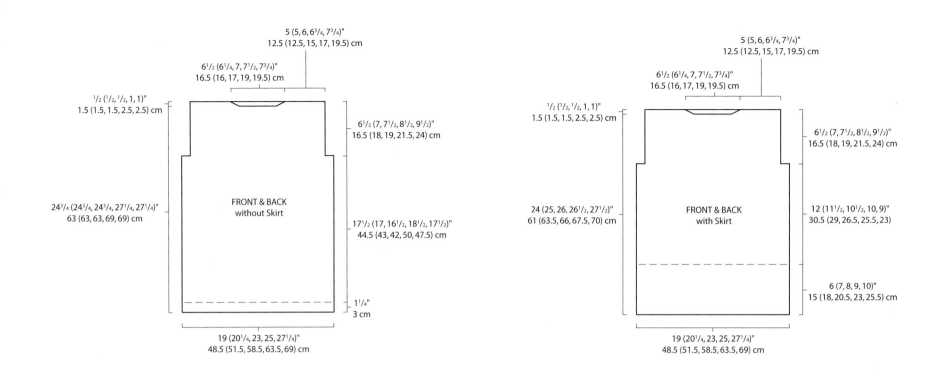

VERSION B: BACK

With smaller straight needle, **CAST ON** 99 (110, 121, 132, 143) sts. Work in Garter Stitch for 8 rows (4 ridges). Work 4 rows of St st, inc 13 (12, 13, 14, 15) sts evenly across the last row, ending 112 (122, 134, 146, 158) sts.

Change to larger needle and work Body pattern same as Version A. When piece measures 18¾ (18¼, 17¾, 19¾, 18¾) inches from the beginning, work underarm shaping as for Version A. Work a total of 8 (8, 8, 9, 9) repeats of Body Chart. Bind off all sts.

VERSION B: FRONT

Work as for Back until piece measures ½ (1½, 1½, 1, 1) inch(es) less than Back. Work neck shaping same as Version A.

SLEEVES (BOTH VERSIONS)

With smaller needle, **CAST ON** 46 (50, 52, 58, 64) sts. Work in Garter Stitch for 8 rows (4 ridges). Work 4 rows of St st, inc 4 (4, 6, 4, 4) sts evenly across last row. There are 50 (54, 58, 62, 68) sts. Change to Size 5 needle and begin Sleeve Chart: Purl 11 (13, 15, 17, 20) sts, work Sleeve Chart over center 28 sts, end p11 (13, 15, 17, 20) sts.

Women's: *At the same time* inc 1 st each end of every 4 rows 7 (5, 17, 18, 24) times, then every 5 rows 18 (20, 12, 12, 8) times for 100 (104, 116, 122, 132) sts on needle. Work even until sleeve measures 17½ (17½, 19½, 19¼, 20¾) inches. Bind off 34 (36, 42, 45, 50) sts at the beginning of the next 2 rows, leaving center 32 sts of pattern for saddle.

Continue working Sleeve Chart over saddle with 2 purl sts each edge. Work 7 (7, 8, 8, 8) reps of Sleeve Chart in total for sleeve, ending with Row 24. Bind off all sts.

Men's: *At the same time* inc 1 st each end of every 5 rows 10 (6, 18, 25, 28) times, then every 6 rows 15 (19, 11, 5, 4) times for 100 (104, 116, 122, 132) sts on needle. Work even until sleeve measures 20½ (20½, 22½, 22¼, 23¾) inches. Bind off 34 (36, 42, 45, 50) sts at the beginning of the next 2 rows, leaving center 32 sts of pattern for saddle. Continue working Sleeve Chart over saddle with 2 purl sts each edge. Work 8 (8, 9, 9, 10) reps of Sleeve Chart in total for sleeve, ending with Row 24. Bind off all sts.

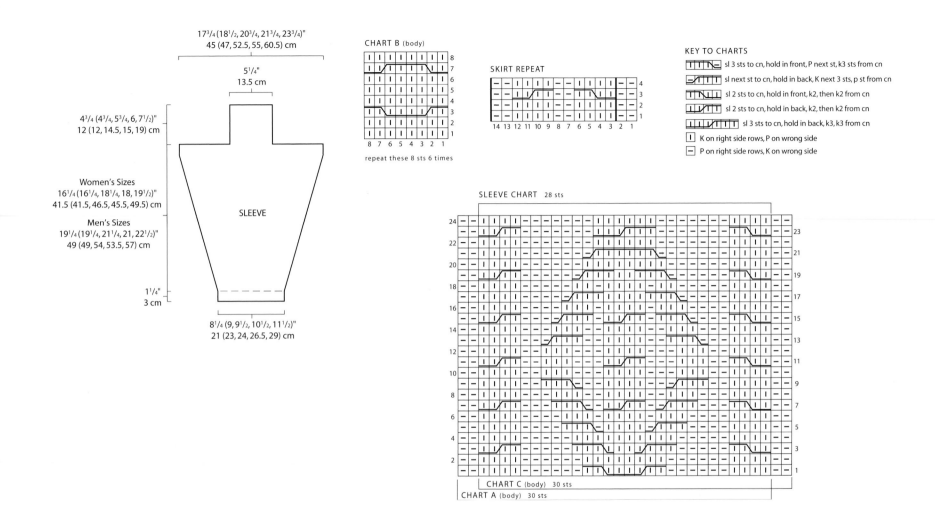

17³⁄₄ (18¹⁄₂, 20³⁄₄, 21³⁄₄, 23³⁄₄)"
45 (47, 52.5, 55, 60.5) cm

5¹⁄₄"
13.5 cm

4³⁄₄ (4³⁄₄, 5³⁄₄, 6, 7¹⁄₂)"
12 (12, 14.5, 15, 19) cm

Women's Sizes
16¹⁄₄ (16¹⁄₄, 18¹⁄₄, 18, 19¹⁄₂)"
41.5 (41.5, 46.5, 45.5, 49.5) cm

Men's Sizes
19¹⁄₄ (19¹⁄₄, 21¹⁄₄, 21, 22¹⁄₂)"
49 (49, 54, 53.5, 57) cm

SLEEVE

1¹⁄₄"
3 cm

8¹⁄₄ (9, 9¹⁄₂, 10¹⁄₂, 11¹⁄₂)"
21 (23, 24, 26.5, 29) cm

CHART B (body)

SKIRT REPEAT

repeat these 8 sts 6 times

KEY TO CHARTS

sl 3 sts to cn, hold in front, P next st, k3 sts from cn
sl next st to cn, hold in back, K next 3 sts, p st from cn
sl 2 sts to cn, hold in front, k2, then k2 from cn
sl 2 sts to cn, hold in back, k2, then k2 from cn
sl 3 sts to cn, hold in back, k3, k3 from cn
I   K on right side rows, P on wrong side
—   P on right side rows, K on wrong side

SLEEVE CHART   28 sts

CHART C (body)   30 sts
CHART A (body)   30 sts

FINISHING

Block carefully to measurements. Sew in saddle; set in sleeve and sew sleeve seam. Sew side seams, leaving Version A skirt open for shirttails.

Neck edging (both versions): Using smaller circular needle, pick up 102 (102, 106, 120, 122) sts evenly around neck edge. Work in Garter Stitch in the round as follows:

Row 1: Purl.
Row 2: Knit.
Alternating these two rows, work for 6 rows, ending with Row 2. Bind off loosely in purl. Weave in loose ends.
For washing instructions read "Caring for Handknits" on page xiv.

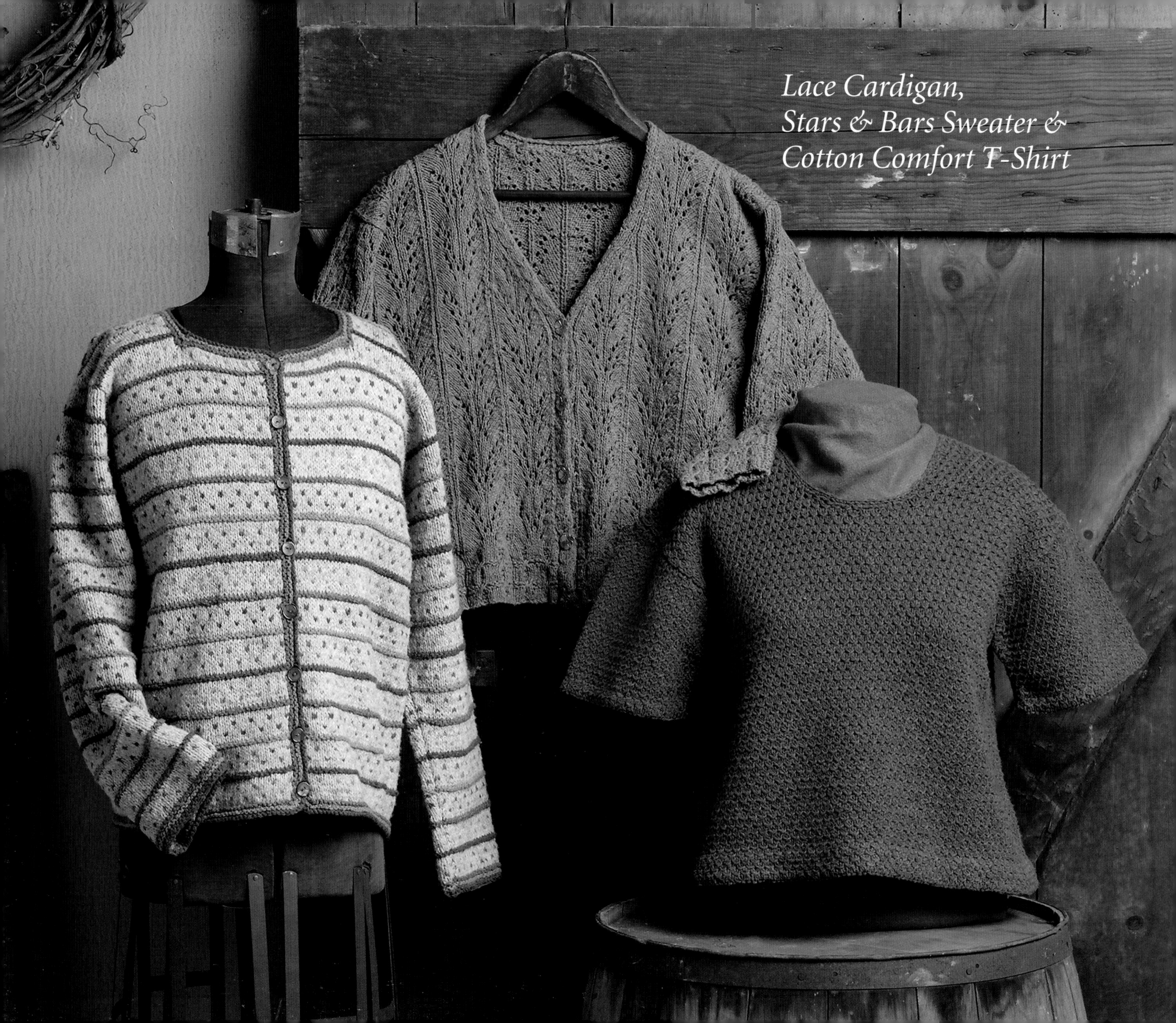
Lace Cardigan,
Stars & Bars Sweater &
Cotton Comfort T-Shirt

LACE CARDIGAN

(Pictured in Weathered Green Cotton Comfort)

Cables and ribbing at the hem and cuffs merge into lace panels separated by vertical ribs. Designer Karen Connor adds a clever continuous cable to form the buttonband and neckband.

An advanced pattern.

SIZES
Petite (Small, Medium, Large)

FINISHED MEASUREMENTS
Chest (buttoned): 37½ (40½, 44, 47½)"/95.5 (103, 112, 120.5) cm
Length: 20 (20½, 21½, 22)"/51 (52, 54, 56) cm

GAUGE
23 sts & 28 rows = 4" (10 cm) in Lace Pattern

MATERIALS
Yarn
Cotton Comfort or Alpaca Elegance: 6 (7, 8, 9) 2 oz skeins
Needles: Size 5 (3.75 mm) 24" (60 cm) or 29" (80 cm) circular; a pair of Size 5 (3.75 mm) or smaller straight needles; cable needle (cn); tapestry needle
Stitch holders: 4 medium, 2 safety pins
Buttons: ⅝"/2.0 cm: 5

RIB PATTERN A (16 ST REPEAT)

Rows 1, 3 & 5 (WS): *P3, k2, p5, k2, p3, k1, repeat from *.
Rows 2, 4 & 6: *P1, k15, repeat from *.
Rows 7 & 9: *K2, sl 1 wyif, k2, sl 1 wyif, k3, sl 1 wyif, k2, sl 1 wyif, k3, repeat from *.
Row 8: *P1, k2, sl 1 wyib, k2, sl 1 wyib, k3, sl 1 wyib, k2, sl 1 wyib, k2, repeat from *.
Row 10: *P1, k2, drop next st from needle to front, sl 2 sts to right needle, drop next st; then pick up first dropped st with left needle, sl 2 sts from right back to left needle, pick up last dropped st with right needle and transfer it to left needle; k7, repeat dropped sts, k6. Repeat from *.

RIB PATTERN B (18 ST REPEAT)

Rows 1, 3 & 5 (WS): *P4, k2, p5, k2, p4, k1, repeat from *.
Rows 2, 4 & 6: *P1, k17, repeat from *.
Rows 7 & 9: *K3, sl 1 wyif, k2, sl 1 wyif, k3, sl 1 wyif, k2, sl 1 wyif, k 4, repeat from *.
Row 8: *P1, k3, sl 1 wyib, k2, sl 1 wyib, k3, sl 1 wyib, k2, sl 1 wyib, k3, repeat from *.
Row 10: *P1, k3, drop next st from needle to front, sl 2 sts to right needle, drop next st; then pick up first dropped st with left needle, sl 2 sts from right back to left needle, pick up last dropped st with right needle and transfer it to left needle; k7, repeat dropped sts, k7. Repeat from *.

CAST ON 223 (239, 259, 279) sts and work Front Cable Bands and Rib Pattern. *(Cable Band directions below are in italics.)* Repeats of the Rib Pattern are worked as follows:

Petite: 1 repeat A, 10 repeats B, 1 repeat A.
Small: 6 repeats A, 2 repeats B, 6 repeats A.
Medium: 1 repeat A, 12 repeats B, 1 repeat A.
Large: 2 repeats A, 1 repeat B, 2 A, 2 B, 2 A, 2 B, 2 A, 1 B, 2 A.
Row 1 (WS): Cable Band k1, p4, k1, pm on needle; work Row 1 of Rib Pattern for your size to within 5 sts of end of row; pm on needle, *Cable Band p4, k1.*
Row 2: P1, cross cable by sl next st to cn and hold in back, k1, knit st from cn, sl next st to cn and hold in front, k1, knit st from cn; work Row 2 of Rib Pattern for your size to within 6 sts of end of row; *p1, cross cable on next 4 sts, p1.*

Buttonholes: The first buttonhole is worked in the following 2 rows. Additional buttonholes are worked every 2½ (2¾, 3, 3¼) inches, for a total of 5 buttonholes.
Row 3: K1, p4, k1; work Row 3 of Rib

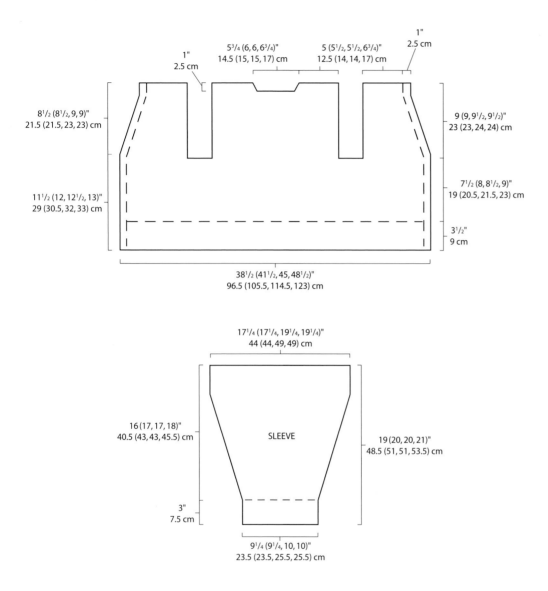

1"
2.5 cm

5³/₄ (6, 6, 6³/₄)"
14.5 (15, 15, 17) cm

5 (5¹/₂, 5¹/₂, 6³/₄)"
12.5 (14, 14, 17) cm

1"
2.5 cm

8¹/₂ (8¹/₂, 9, 9)"
21.5 (21.5, 23, 23) cm

9 (9, 9¹/₂, 9¹/₂)"
23 (23, 24, 24) cm

11¹/₂ (12, 12¹/₂, 13)"
29 (30.5, 32, 33) cm

7¹/₂ (8, 8¹/₂, 9)"
19 (20.5, 21.5, 23) cm

3¹/₂"
9 cm

38¹/₂ (41¹/₂, 45, 48¹/₂)"
96.5 (105.5, 114.5, 123) cm

17¹/₄ (17¹/₄, 19¹/₄, 19¹/₄)"
44 (44, 49, 49) cm

16 (17, 17, 18)"
40.5 (43, 43, 45.5) cm

SLEEVE

19 (20, 20, 21)"
48.5 (51, 51, 53.5) cm

3"
7.5 cm

9¹/₄ (9¹/₄, 10, 10)"
23.5 (23.5, 25.5, 25.5) cm

Pattern for your size to within last 5 sts;
*p1, bind off the following 2 sts, knit the
last st.*
Row 4: P1, k1, cast on 2 sts, k1; work Row 4
of Rib Pattern for your size to within last
6 sts; *p1, k 4, p1.*
Row 5: K1, p4, k1; work Row 5 of Rib

Pattern for your size to within 5 sts of end
of row; *p4, k1.*
Row 6: P1, k4; work Row 6 of Rib Pattern
for your size to within last 6 sts; *p1, k4,
p1.*
Repeat the 6 rows for the Cable Bands
while continuing the Rib Pattern. Work

the 10 rows of Rib Pattern 2 times, and
then work Rows 1 through 6 of the Rib
Pattern again.

Lace Pattern B: On the following row, continue working Cable Bands as established,
and begin Lace Pattern from charts on page
67. Repeats of Lace Pattern charts are
worked as follows:
Petite: 1 repeat A, 10 repeats B, 1 repeat A.
Small: 6 repeats A, 2 repeats B, 6 repeats A.
Medium: 1 repeat A, 12 repeats B, 1 repeat A.
Large: 2 repeats A, 1 repeat B, 2 A, 2 B, 2 A,
2 B, 2 A, 1 B, 2 A.

Continue to work Cable Bands (remembering to place buttonholes) and the 18 rows of
Lace Pattern until entire piece measures 11
(11½, 12, 12½) inches, or desired length to
underarm, having finished a RS row.

DIVIDE FOR FRONT AND BACK
Work across 49 (53, 57, 62) sts for Left
Front and place these sts on a holder or
scrap yarn; bind off 17 (17, 19, 19) sts, work
across next 91 (99, 107, 117) sts for Back.
Place rem 66 (70, 76, 81) sts on a holder or
scrap yarn.

BACK
Continue working in established pattern
until armhole measures 8 (8, 8½, 8½)
inches, having completed a WS row. On the
following row, work 32 (35, 39, 42) sts for
right shoulder, bind off center 27 (29, 29,
33) sts, complete row for left shoulder.
Working each shoulder separately, dec 1 st at
neck edge every other row 3 times. Work 1

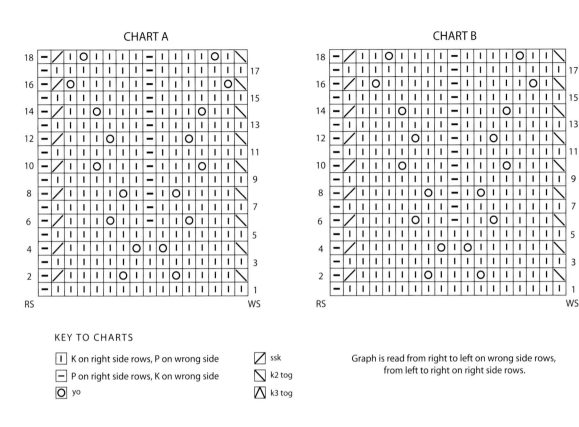

CHART A

CHART B

Graph is read from right to left on wrong side rows,
from left to right on right side rows.

KEY TO CHARTS

I	K on right side rows, P on wrong side
-	P on right side rows, K on wrong side
O	yo
⟋	ssk
⟍	k2 tog
⟋⟍	k3 tog

row even. Slip rem 29 (32, 36, 39) shoulder sts onto holders.

LEFT FRONT

Transfer sts from holder to needle and join yarn at armhole. Beginning with a RS row, work 4 rows in patts as established. On the following row, work in patt to last 8 sts, k2tog, work Cable Band. Decrease as follows:

• Every other row 6 (7, 7, 8) times
• Every fourth row 6 (6, 6, 8) times
• Every sixth row 2 (2, 2, 1) times

There are 35 (38, 42, 45) sts. Continue in patt until Front measures same as Back. Place sts on holder or scrap yarn.

RIGHT FRONT

Transfer sts from holder to needle and join yarn at armhole. Bind off 17 (17, 19, 19) sts and complete row. There are 49 (53, 57, 62) sts. Work 4 rows in patts as established. Make neck dec to correspond to Left Front. Decrease rows will be: Work Cable Band, p1, k2tog, complete row in established pattern.

JOIN SHOULDERS

Transfer the 6 sts for Cable Bands to safety pins. Join shoulders using the Three Needle Bind Off method, RS together.

SLEEVES

CAST ON 53 (53, 57, 57) sts.

Row 1: P0 (0, 2, 2), k3 (3, 3, 3); work 3 repeats of Row 1 (48 sts) Rib Pattern A; then k2 (2, 2, 2), p0 (0, 2, 2).

Row 2: K2 (2, 4, 4) sts, work 3 repeats Row 2 of Rib Pattern A; then p1, k2 (2, 4, 4) sts.

Continue in this manner for 24 more rows. On the following row, work the first row of Lace Pattern Chart A over the 48 sts of Rib Pattern and work the additional sts in St st.

Then begin to inc, incorporating new sts into the Lace Pattern as able. *NB: Do not work the k2tog or the ssk unless there is space to also do the corresponding yo!*

Increase 1 st each end of row as follows:

• Every row 3 (3, 3, 3) times
• Every other row 6 (3, 7, 7) times
• Every fourth row 6 (8, 9, 9) times
• Every sixth row 8 (9, 8, 8) times

There are 99 (99, 111, 111) sts. Continue in patt until sleeve measures 19 (20, 20, 21) inches, or desired length from beginning. Bind off loosely.

CABLE TRIM

Slip the 6 sts for Cable Band on Right Front onto needle. Continue Cable Band across the back by picking up and working

1 bound off st from Back Neck together with the first or last st of Cable Band.

RS rows: Work 5 sts as usual; bring yarn to front; slip sixth st to right needle as if to purl; pick up next st along neck edge with left needle as if to purl; transfer sixth st back to left needle. Purl these 2 sts together.

WS rows: Wyib, pick up st along neck as if to knit, leave on right needle; knit first st from Cable Band; pass picked up st over knit st and pull yarn firm. Finish row.

NB: In order to end at an appropriate row to join with Front Band sts on Left Front, you may need to adjust slightly the number of sts picked up along Back neck edge.

When trim has been worked across Back neck, graft these sts to the 6 sts from Left Front as follows:

Transfer each group of 6 sts onto straight needles and weave the two sides together using the Kitchener Stitch.

FINISHING
Sew sleeves in place. Sew side and sleeve seams. Sew on buttons. Weave in loose ends.

For washing instructions read "Caring for Handknits" on page xiv.

STARS & BARS CARDIGAN AND PULLOVER

(Adult cardigan on page 64 pictured in Unbleached White, Violet, Weathered Green, and Denim Cotton Comfort; Child cardigan pictured on page 76 in Peony, Maize, Bluet, and Yarrow Cotton Comfort)

This four-color pattern uses only two colors at a time. Styled as a pullover or cardigan, it is sized for children and adults. Multicolor Garter Stitch borders add interest at the cuffs, hem, and mitred neckline.

An intermediate pattern.

SIZES
Child: 2 (4, 6, 8, 10)
Adult: 36 (40, 44, 48, 52)

FINISHED MEASUREMENTS
Chest: Child: 24 (26, 28, 30, 32)"/61 (66, 71, 76, 81.5) cm. **Adult:** 36 (40, 44, 48, 52)"/91.5 (101.5, 112, 122, 132) cm.
Length to shoulder: Child: 11½ (12½, 13½, 15, 17)"/ 29 (32, 34.5, 38, 43) cm. **Adult:** 21 (22, 24, 25, 26)"/53.5 (56, 61, 63.5, 66) cm.
Sleeve: Child: 9 (10, 11, 12, 13)"/23 (25.5, 28, 30.5, 33) cm. **Adult:** 18 (19, 20, 21, 22)"/45.5 (48.5, 51, 53.5, 56) cm.

GAUGE
5 sts & 10 rows = 1¼" (3.0 cm) using Size 7 needle in PS

MATERIALS
Yarn
Cotton Comfort or Alpaca Elegance:
Child: 3 (4, 4, 5, 5) 2 oz skeins main color (MC). **Adult:** 7 (7, 8, 10, 11) 2 oz skeins Main Color (MC). **Child & Adult:** 1 2 oz skein each of 3 colors (A, B, C).
Needles: Child: Sizes 5 (3.75 mm) & 7 (4.5 mm) 24"(60 cm) circular; Size 5 (3.75 mm) dpn. **Adult:** Sizes 5 (3.75 mm) & 7 (4.5 mm) 29" (80 cm) circular; Size 5 (3.75 mm) dpn.
Stitch holders: 1 large, 3 medium
Buttons (cardigan): Child: 6 (6, 6, 7, 7) ½"/1.5 cm. **Adult:** 7 (8, 8, 9, 10) ⅝"/1.25 cm.

PULLOVER
CAST ON 120 (132, 140, 152, 160) sts for Child, 180 (200, 220, 240, 260) sts for Adult, using Color A and smaller circular needle. Join sts, making sure sts are not twisted on needle. Purl 1 round Color A. With Color B, k1 round, p1 round. With Color C, k1 round, p1 round. Change to larger needle and work Pullover Chart. Knit all rounds except Rounds 10, 20, and 30, which are purled for a Garter Stitch ridge on RS of work. Continue in patt until entire piece measures 6½ (7, 7½, 8½, 10) inches for Child, 12 (12½, 14, 14½, 15) inches for Adult, or desired length to underarm. If your last round is a number ending in 8 (4, 8, 0, 6), e.g., 8 (14, 18, 20, 26), or 2 (6, 0, 4, 8), e.g., 12 (16, 20, 24, 28), and you have a row gauge of 10 rows/1¼ inches, then you will have a Garter Stitch ridge at the shoulder line.

Divide for Armholes: Bind off 3 (4, 4, 4, 4) underarm sts for Child, 8 (10, 10, 10, 15) underarm sts for Adult. Knit 54 (58, 62, 68, 72) sts for Child, 74 (80, 90, 100, 100) sts for Adult for Back; place rem sts on large holder. *NB: To continue in patt, RS rows will be knit, WS rows will be purl, except Rows 10, 20, and 30, which will now be knit rows.*

CARDIGAN
CAST ON 121 (133, 141, 153, 161) sts for Child, 181 (201, 221, 241, 261) sts for Adult, using MC and larger needle. In St st, work Cardigan Chart. *NB: Rows 10, 20, and 30 are knit instead of purl for a Garter Stitch ridge on RS of work.* Continue in patt until entire piece measures 6 (6½, 7, 8, 9½)

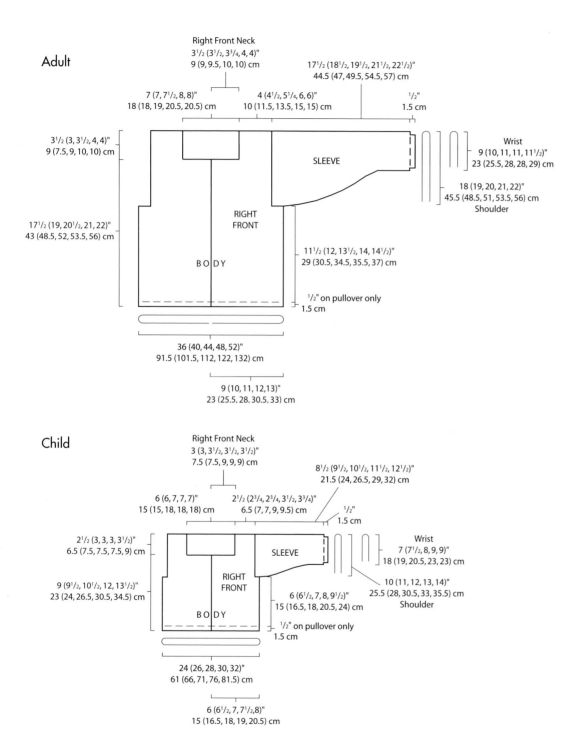

Adult

Right Front Neck
3½ (3½, 3¾, 4, 4)"
9 (9, 9.5, 10, 10) cm

17½ (18½, 19½, 21½, 22½)"
44.5 (47, 49.5, 54.5, 57) cm

7 (7, 7½, 8, 8)"
18 (18, 19, 20.5, 20.5) cm

4 (4½, 5¼, 6, 6)"
10 (11.5, 13.5, 15, 15) cm

½"
1.5 cm

3½ (3, 3½, 4, 4)"
9 (7.5, 9, 10, 10) cm

SLEEVE

Wrist
9 (10, 11, 11, 11½)"
23 (25.5, 28, 28, 29) cm

18 (19, 20, 21, 22)"
45.5 (48.5, 51, 53.5, 56) cm
Shoulder

RIGHT
FRONT

17½ (19, 20½, 21, 22)"
43 (48.5, 52, 53.5, 56) cm

11½ (12, 13½, 14, 14½)"
29 (30.5, 34.5, 35.5, 37) cm

BODY

½" on pullover only
1.5 cm

36 (40, 44, 48, 52)"
91.5 (101.5, 112, 122, 132) cm

9 (10, 11, 12, 13)"
23 (25.5, 28, 30.5, 33) cm

Child

Right Front Neck
3 (3, 3½, 3½, 3½)"
7.5 (7.5, 9, 9, 9) cm

8½ (9½, 10½, 11½, 12½)"
21.5 (24, 26.5, 29, 32) cm

6 (6, 7, 7, 7)"
15 (15, 18, 18, 18) cm

2½ (2¾, 2¾, 3½, 3¾)"
6.5 (7, 7, 9, 9.5) cm

½"
1.5 cm

2½ (3, 3, 3½)"
6.5 (7.5, 7.5, 7.5, 9) cm

SLEEVE

Wrist
7 (7½, 8, 9, 9)"
18 (19, 20.5, 23, 23) cm

10 (11, 12, 13, 14)"
25.5 (28, 30.5, 33, 35.5) cm
Shoulder

9 (9½, 10½, 12, 13½)"
23 (24, 26.5, 30.5, 34.5) cm

RIGHT
FRONT

6 (6½, 7, 8, 9½)"
15 (16.5, 18, 20.5, 24) cm

BODY

½" on pullover only
1.5 cm

24 (26, 28, 30, 32)"
61 (66, 71, 76, 81.5) cm

6 (6½, 7, 7½, 8)"
15 (16.5, 18, 19, 20.5) cm

inches for Child, 11½ (12, 13½, 14, 14½) inches for Adult, or ½ inch less than desired length to underarm. (The Garter Stitch border, added later, will inc the length by ½ inch.) If your last round is a number ending in 0 (4, 8, 2, 6), e.g. 10 (14, 18, 22, 26), and you have a row gauge of 10 rows/1¼ inches, then you will have a Garter Stitch ridge at the shoulder line, for an attractive finish.

Divide for Armholes: Work 27 (29, 31, 34, 36) sts for Child, 35 (40, 45, 50, 50) sts for Adult; place these sts on a holder for Right Front. Bind off 6 (8, 8, 8, 8) underarm sts for Child, 16 (20, 20, 20, 30) underarm sts for Adult. Work 54 (58, 62, 68, 72) sts for Child, 74 (80, 90, 100, 100) sts for Adult for Back; place rem sts on large holder for Left Front. *NB: There will be one more st for Left Front than for Right Front.*

PULLOVER AND CARDIGAN BACK

Keeping in patt, work until armhole measures 5 (5½, 6, 6½, 7) inches for Child, 9 (9½, 10, 10½, 11) inches for Adult, ending with Row 10, 20, or 30, if possible. On the following row, work 12 (14, 14, 17, 19) sts for Child, 20 (22, 26, 30, 30) sts for Adult, and place these sts on a holder for Right Shoulder; bind off 30 (30, 34, 34, 34) sts for Child, 34 (36, 38, 40, 40) sts for Adult, for Neck; purl rem 12 (14, 14, 17, 19) sts for Child, 20 (22, 26, 30, 30) sts for Adult, and place them on a holder for Left Shoulder.

PULLOVER FRONT

Beginning with a RS row, bind off 6 (8, 8, 8, 8) underarm sts for Child, 16 (20, 20, 20,

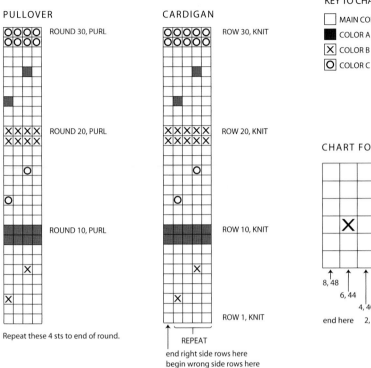

PULLOVER

ROUND 30, PURL

ROUND 20, PURL

ROUND 10, PURL

Repeat these 4 sts to end of round.

CARDIGAN

ROW 30, KNIT

ROW 20, KNIT

ROW 10, KNIT

ROW 1, KNIT

REPEAT

end right side rows here
begin wrong side rows here

KEY TO CHART

☐ MAIN COLOR
■ COLOR A
☒ COLOR B
⊙ COLOR C

CHART FOR SLEEVE

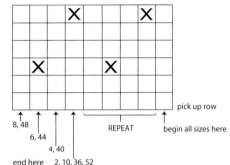

pick up row

REPEAT

begin all sizes here

8, 48

6, 44

4, 40

end here   2, 10, 36, 52

30) underarm sts for Adult. Knit 54 (58, 62, 68, 72) sts for Child, 74 (80, 90, 100, 100) sts for Adult, and bind off rem 3 (4, 4, 4, 4) sts for Child, 8 (10, 10, 10, 15) sts for Adult. Work until armhole measures 2½ (2½, 3, 3½, 3½) inches for Child, 5½ (6½, 6½, 6½, 7) inches for Adult, having completed a WS row.

Neck Shaping: Work 12 (14, 14, 17, 19) sts for Child, 20 (22, 26, 30, 30) sts for Adult, for Right Front and put these sts on a holder. Bind off 30 (30, 34, 34, 34) sts for Child, 34 (36, 38, 40, 40) sts for Adult for Neck; work rem 12 (14, 14, 17, 17) sts for

Child, 20 (22, 26, 30, 30) sts for Adult, for Left Front.

Continue working Left Front in patt until armhole measures same as for Back, ending with Row 8, 18, or 28, if possible. Place sts on a medium holder. Transfer sts for Right Front from holder to needle and work to correspond to Left Front.

CARDIGAN FRONT

Transfer sts for Right Front from holder to needle and, beginning with a RS row, work in patt until armhole measures 2½ (2½, 3, 3½, 3½) inches for Child, 5½ (6½, 6½,

6½, 7) inches for Adult, having completed a WS row. At the beginning of the next row, bind off 15 (15, 17, 17, 17) sts for Child, 17 (18, 19, 20, 20) sts for Adult, for neck. Work rem 12 (14, 14, 17, 19) sts for Child, 20 (22, 26, 30, 30) sts for Adult, until armhole measures same as for Back, ending with Row 8, 18, or 28 if possible. Place sts on a medium holder.

Transfer rem sts for Left Front from holder to needle. Beginning with a WS row, bind off 6 (8, 8, 8, 8) underarm sts for Child, 16 (20, 20, 20, 30) underarm sts for Adult.

Continue to work to correspond to Right Front. The bound off sts for neck will be on a WS row, and will be 16 (16, 18, 18, 18) sts for Child, 18 (19, 20, 21, 21) sts for Adult, one more than for Right Front.

PULLOVER AND CARDIGAN: JOIN SHOULDERS

Turn body of sweater WS out. With RS together, join shoulders using the Three Needle Bind Off method. Turn work RS facing out.

SLEEVES

With RS of work facing you, with MC, pick up and k50 (55, 60, 65, 70) sts for Child, 90 (95, 100, 105, 110) sts for Adult, along armhole edge, being sure to pick up 1 st at each bump made by Garter Stitch ridge. The sleeves are knit back and forth. Work the first 6 rows using Sleeve Chart.

Continue in patt as for Body of sweater,

remembering to knit Rows 10, 20, and 30. Dec 1 st at beginning and end of row every inch 6 times. Continue to dec every ½ inch 1 (1, 2, 1, 4) more time(s) for Child, 14 (14, 14, 14, 15, 17) more times for Adult. There are 36 (41, 44, 49, 50) sts for Child, 50 (55, 60, 63, 64) sts for Adult. Work even until sleeve measures 8½ (9½, 10½, 11½, 12½) inches for Child, 19½ (20½, 21½, 22½, 23½) inches for Adult, ½ inch less than desired length to cuff. In the following row, dec evenly 2 (4, 4, 5, 5) times for Child, 5 (5, 6, 7, 7) times for Adult. Change to smaller (Size 5) needles and work Garter Stitch cuff as follows:

Color C: Knit 2 rows.
Color B: Knit 2 rows.
Color A: Knit 2 rows, binding off all sts while knitting.

Repeat for second sleeve.

PULLOVER NECK

Work Garter Stitch band around neck as follows: Using Color C, smaller dpn needles, and with RS of work facing, pick up and k30 (30, 34, 34, 34) bound off sts for Child, 36 (36, 38, 40, 41) bound off sts for Adult, for Back neck; pick up and k7 sts for every 10 rows, including one st at each Garter stitch bump along left side of neck; pick up and k30 (30, 34, 34, 34) bound off sts for Child, 36 (36, 38, 40, 41) bound off sts for Adult, for Front neck; pick up and k7 sts for every 10 rows, including one st at each Garter stitch bump along RS of neck.

Round 1: Using Color C, purl all sts.
Round 2: Using Color B, knit all sts, and dec 2 sts at each of the 4 corners of neck.
Round 3: Using Color B, purl all sts.
Round 4: Using Color A, knit all sts, and dec 2 sts at each of the 4 corners of neck.
Round 5: Using Color A, purl all sts.
Round 6: Using Color A, bind off while knitting, and dec 2 sts at each of 4 corners of neck.

CARDIGAN NECK

Work Garter stitch band around Right Front of sweater as follows: With RS of work facing, using Color C and smaller circular needle, begin at center Back. Pick up and k60 (66, 70, 76, 80) sts for Child, 90 (100, 110, 120, 130) sts for Adult, along bottom edge of sweater; pm on needle. Pick up and k7 sts for every 10 rows, including one st at each Garter Stitch bump along Right Front edge; pm on needle. Pick up and k15 (15, 17, 17, 17) bound off sts for Child, 18 (18, 19, 20, 21) bound off sts for Adult, for neck; pm on needle. Pick up and k7 sts for every 10 rows, including one st at each Garter stitch bump along side of neck, pm on needle. Pick up and k15 (15, 17, 17, 17) bound off sts for Child, 17 (18, 19, 20, 20) bound off sts for Adult, to center of Back neck. Work back and forth, knitting each row as follows:

Row 1: Using Color C, dec 1 st each side of first 2 markers; inc 1 st each side of the following 2 markers.
Row 2: Using Color B, knit all sts without any inc or dec.
Row 3: Using Color B, work as for Row 1. For a girl's or woman's sweater, work 6 (6, 6, 7, 7) buttonholes for Child, 7 (8, 8, 9, 10) for Adult evenly spaced along Right Front edge. Bind off 2 sts for each buttonhole.
Row 4: Using Color A, knit all sts, casting on 2 sts at each buttonhole.
Row 5: Using Color A, inc and dec as for Row 1, and at the same time, bind off all sts.

Work Garter Stitch band around Left Front of sweater. Beginning at center Back of neck, pick up and knit sts around neck, along Front, and along bottom edge to center Back, placing markers and working to correspond to band for Right Front of sweater. For a boy's or man's sweater, work buttonholes along Left Front in second and third row.

FINISHING

Join Garter Stitch seams at center neck and center hem. Being careful to make square corner, sew upper sleeve edge to cast off sts at bottom of the armhole. Sew sleeve seams. Weave in loose ends.

For washing instructions read "Caring for Handknits" on page xiv.

COTTON COMFORT T-SHIRT

(Pictured in Violet Cotton Comfort on page 64)

In designing this cropped three-season shirt, Spinnery friend Rebecca Rothfusz combined her fondness for Cotton Comfort with the need for a summer pullover. The all-over textured Grecian Plait Stitch (from Barbara G. Walker's *A Treasury of Knitting Patterns*) is fun to learn and do, and set off neatly by a turned-under hem and crochet neckline. Choose short or three-quarter-length sleeves.

An intermediate pattern.

SIZES
Petite (Small, Medium, Large, X-Large)

FINISHED MEASUREMENTS
Chest: 36 (40, 44, 48, 52)"/ 91.5 (101.5, 112, 122, 132) cm
Length to shoulder: 19¼ (20¼, 21¼, 23¾, 25¼)"/49 (51.5, 54, 59, 64) cm
Sleeve: Short version to armhole: 4 (4½, 5, 5½, 6)"/10 (11.5, 12.5, 14, 15) cm. **Three-quarter length to armhole:** 11 (12, 12½, 13, 13½)"/28 (30.5, 32, 33, 34.5) cm.

GAUGE
16 sts = 3" (7.5 cm)

MATERIALS
Yarn: Cotton Comfort, Alpaca Elegance, or Sylvan Spirit
Short sleeves: 5 (5, 6, 7, 8) 2 oz skeins.
¾ sleeves: 6 (6, 7, 8, 9) 2 oz skeins.
Needles: Sizes 5, 7, 10 (3.75, 4.5, 6.0 mm) straight needles (referred to as Sm, Med, or Lg), or sizes needed to obtain gauge
Crochet hook: Size C
Stitch holders: 3 medium
Markers: 8 small safety pins

TEST SWATCH
Before you begin: Read through and knit the test swatch to familiarize yourself with the Grecian Plait Stitch. Then, knit away!

HOW TO WORK "K SECOND ST OVER, K1 ST":
This technique is tricky to describe but easy to do. Your objective is to knit the second st on the lh needle first, and then to pick it up and pull it off the lh needle and onto the rh needle over the first st, which has not been knit yet. Here are two methods:

1. Insert point of rh needle as if to purl into the second st, lift this st over the first st, and lay it down nearer the needle point, in front of the first st. Knit the second st from this position and transfer it to rh needle. Then knit the first st.

2. Keeping the rh needle in front of the lh needle, knit second st through the front of the loop, then lift it over the first st and off lh to rh needle. Knit first st.

With Lg needle, cast on 20 sts. Work Grecian Plait Pattern as follows:

Grecian Plait Pattern
NB: The pattern includes 2 selvage sts at each end of row.
Row 1: RS (all RS rows, use Med needle): Slip first st knitwise, p1, knit to last 2 sts, p1, k1.
Row 2 & 4: WS (all WS rows use Lg needle): Slip first st purlwise, k1, p to last 2 sts, k1, p1.
Row 3: Slip first st knitwise, p1, *knit second st over, k1, repeat from * across to last 2 sts; p1, k1.

Row 5: Slip first st knitwise, p1, k1, *knit second st over, k1, repeat from* across to last 3 sts; k1, p1, k1.
Repeat Rows 2 through 5.

After 24 rows, bind off loosely on a RS row, in patt.

After washing and blocking, the test swatch should measure 3 inches square, not counting the 4 selvage sts.

BACK
Using Lg needle, **CAST ON** 98 (108, 118, 130, 140) sts. Work hem as follows: With Sm needles, work 5 rows St st. Change to Med needle, k1 row to make Garter stitch ridge or "turning" row. Work Grecian Plait Pattern for the first 5 rows using Sm needle for RS rows and Med needle for WS rows.

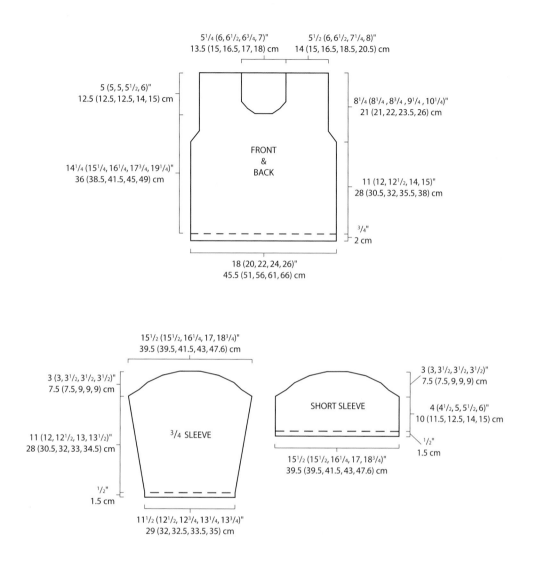

5¼ (6, 6½, 6¾, 7)"
13.5 (15, 16.5, 17, 18) cm

5½ (6, 6½, 7¼, 8)"
14 (15, 16.5, 18.5, 20.5) cm

5 (5, 5, 5½, 6)"
12.5 (12.5, 12.5, 14, 15) cm

8¼ (8¼, 8¾, 9¼, 10¼)"
21 (21, 22, 23.5, 26) cm

FRONT
&
BACK

14¼ (15¼, 16¼, 17¾, 19¼)"
36 (38.5, 41.5, 45, 49) cm

11 (12, 12½, 14, 15)"
28 (30.5, 32, 35.5, 38) cm

¾"
2 cm

18 (20, 22, 24, 26)"
45.5 (51, 56, 61, 66) cm

15½ (15½, 16¼, 17, 18¾)"
39.5 (39.5, 41.5, 43, 47.6) cm

3 (3, 3½, 3½, 3½)"
7.5 (7.5, 9, 9, 9) cm

¾ SLEEVE

11 (12, 12½, 13, 13½)"
28 (30.5, 32, 33, 34.5) cm

½"
1.5 cm

11½ (12½, 12¾, 13¼, 13¾)"
29 (32, 32.5, 33.5, 35) cm

3 (3, 3½, 3½, 3½)"
7.5 (7.5, 9, 9, 9) cm

SHORT SLEEVE

4 (4½, 5, 5½, 6)"
10 (11.5, 12.5, 14, 15) cm

½"
1.5 cm

15½ (15½, 16¼, 17, 18¾)"
39.5 (39.5, 41.5, 43, 47.6) cm

Continue in patt using Med needle for RS rows and Lg needle for WS rows. Work 11 (12, 12½, 14, 15) inches from turning row; place small safety pins at each end of this row. On WS, in patt area (not selvage), dec 2 sts at each end of row by p2tog twice. Repeat every fourth row 2 (2, 3, 3, 3) more times. You now have 86 (96, 102, 114, 124) sts. *Work 7 (7, 7, 7½, 8½) inches from the

last dec, ending with a WS row.

Work across and place 29 (32, 34, 39, 43) sts on holder for shoulder, bind off 28 (32, 34, 36, 38) sts for Back neck, work 29 (32, 34, 39, 43) sts and place on holder.

FRONT

Work same as for Back to *. Work 2 (2, 2, 2,

2½) inches above underarm dec, ending with a WS row.

Neck shaping: Work across 37 (42, 44, 50, 54) sts for Left Front. Put these sts on a holder. Bind off center 12 (12, 14, 14, 16) sts. Work across rem 37 (42, 44, 50, 54) sts for Right Front. Work a WS row. Then bind off 4 (4, 4, 5, 5) sts at the neck edge. On the following row, dec 1 st at neck edge and then every 3 rows 3 (5, 5, 5, 5) more times. There are 29 (32, 34, 39, 43) sts. Work until armhole measures same as Back armhole. Put these sts on a holder. Attach yarn and work across WS of Left Front. Shape neck edge to correspond to Right Front.

SLEEVES

Three-quarter sleeve: CAST ON 62 (66, 68, 70, 74) sts. Work hem as for bottom of Back, except work only 3 rows St st with Sm needle. After turning row, work Grecian Plait Pattern using Sm and Med needles for next 4 rows; continue in patt using Med and Lg needles for remainder of sleeve. Increase 1 st at each end of Row 5 and every 4 (6, 6, 6, 5) rows 9 (7, 8, 9, 12) more times. You now have 82 (82, 86, 90, 100) sts. Work until sleeve measures 11 (12, 12½, 13, 13½) inches, or desired length to underarm; mark each end of this row with small safety pins.

Short sleeve: CAST ON 82 (82, 86, 90, 100) sts. Work hem as for bottom of Back except work only 3 rows St st with Sm needle. After turning row, work Grecian Plait Pattern using Sm and Med needles for next

4 rows; continue in patt using Med and Lg needles for remainder of sleeve. Work until sleeve measures 4 (4½, 5, 5½, 6) inches, or desired length to underarm; mark each end of this row with small safety pins.

For three-quarter sleeve and short sleeve:
Decrease 2 sts at each end of next row. Repeat every fourth row 2 (2, 3, 3, 3) more times. You now have 70 (70, 70, 74, 84) sts. Slipping the first st of each row, bind off in patt 4 (4, 4, 1, 1) sts at the beginning of next 2 rows. Then bind off 5 (5, 5, 6, 7) sts at the beginning of the next 10 rows. Bind off rem 12 sts.

JOIN SHOULDERS
Knit shoulders together using the Three Needle Bind Off method and Size 7 needle.

FINISHING
Turn work RS out. Set in sleeves, matching underarm markers. Sew side seams by catching half of each edge st, weaving back and forth between corresponding sts. Work a firm row of sc around neck. Loosely sew hems to inside. Weave in loose ends.

For washing instructions read "Caring for Handknits" on page xiv.

*Rebecca's Little Sweater,
Baby Bonnets, and
Stars & Bars Sweater*

REBECCA'S LITTLE SWEATER

(Pictured in Unbleached White Cotton Comfort)

A neck opening with buttons on both sides guarantees easy "on and off" wear. The brocade pattern provides a delicate texture in this straightforward pullover worked in four pieces.

An intermediate pattern.

SIZES
1 (2, 4, 6)

FINISHED MEASUREMENTS
Chest: 22¼ (25, 27, 29½)"/56.5 (63.5, 68.5, 75) cm
Length to underarm: 6½ (8½, 10½, 12)"/16.5 (21.5, 26.5, 30.5) cm
Sleeve: 6¾ (8¼, 9¾, 11¼)"/17 (21, 25, 28.5) cm
Depth of armhole: 4 (5, 5½, 6½)"/10 (12.5, 14, 16.5) cm

GAUGE
20 sts & 28 rows = 4" (10 cm)

MATERIALS
Yarn
Cotton Comfort or Granite State Green: 2 (3, 4, 5) 2 oz skeins
Needles: Size 6 (4.0 mm) straight, or size required to obtain gauge
Buttons: 6 (6, 6, 8) ½"/1.5 cm
Safety pins: 2 small

BACK
CAST ON 57 (63, 69, 75) sts and work 6 (6, 8, 8) rows of Garter stitch (knit each row). Begin patt as in chart on next row, and work until entire piece measures 6½ (8½, 10½, 12) inches.

ARMHOLE
Bind off 5 (5, 6, 6) sts at the beginning of next 2 rows, and continue working in patt until armhole measures 3¼ (4¼, 4¾, 5¾) inches, ending with a WS row. On the following row work in patt across 12 (14, 14, 17) sts, pm on needle, k23 (25, 29, 29) sts, pm on needle, work rem 12 (14, 14, 17) sts

---

Modern Heirlooms—The contemporary colors and classic textures of three children's projects are destined to be enjoyed now and handed down to the next generation. Cotton Comfort offers easy knitting and cozy wearability.

in patt. For the next 5 rows continue to work the center 23 (25, 29, 29) sts in Garter stitch, keeping the rest of the sts in patt. Place a small safety pin at each end of fifth row. These pins mark the top of each shoulder.

NECK
Work across 12 (14, 14, 17) sts, work 3 (3, 4, 4) sts in Garter stitch. Place these sts on holder for right shoulder. Bind off the following 17 (19, 21, 21) sts for neck. Work 3 (3, 4, 4) sts in Garter stitch and rem sts in patt for left shoulder. Work straight until left shoulder measures 3½ inches from small safety pin. Bind off. Work right shoulder to correspond.

FRONT
CAST ON 57 (63, 69, 75) sts and work to armhole as for Back. Bind off for armholes, and continue in patt until armhole measures

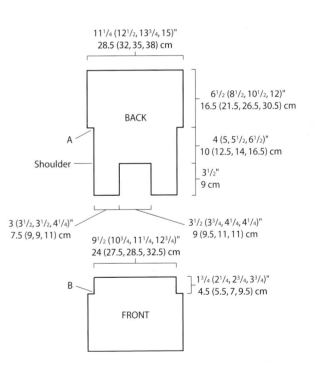

11¼ (12½, 13¾, 15)"
28.5 (32, 35, 38) cm

6½ (8½, 10½, 12)"
16.5 (21.5, 26.5, 30.5) cm

BACK

A

Shoulder

4 (5, 5½, 6½)"
10 (12.5, 14, 16.5) cm

3½"
9 cm

3 (3½, 3½, 4¼)"
7.5 (9, 9, 11) cm

3½ (3¾, 4¼, 4¼)"
9 (9.5, 11, 11) cm

9½ (10¾, 11¼, 12¾)"
24 (27.5, 28.5, 32.5) cm

B

1¾ (2¼, 2¾, 3¾)"
4.5 (5.5, 7, 9.5) cm

FRONT

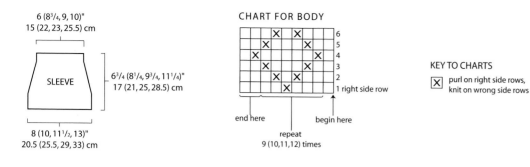

6 (8³/₄, 9, 10)"
15 (22, 23, 25.5) cm

SLEEVE

6³/₄ (8¹/₄, 9³/₄, 11¹/₄)"
17 (21, 25, 28.5) cm

8 (10, 11¹/₂, 13)"
20.5 (25.5, 29, 33) cm

CHART FOR BODY

6
5
4
3
2
1 right side row

end here   begin here

repeat
9 (10, 11, 12) times

KEY TO CHARTS

☒ purl on right side rows,
    knit on wrong side rows

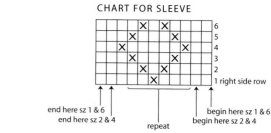

CHART FOR SLEEVE

6
5
4
3
2
1 right side row

end here sz 1 & 6
end here sz 2 & 4

repeat

begin here sz 1 & 6
begin here sz 2 & 4

1 (1½, 2, 3) inches (or slightly more), having completed a RS row. Work 3 rows Garter stitch. On the following row work buttonholes.

BUTTONHOLES

K3, *yo, k2tog, k3 (4, 4, 3), repeat from * 1 (1, 1, 2) time(s), yo, k2tog, k18 (20, 24, 24), *yo, k2tog, k3 (4, 4, 3), repeat from * 1 (1, 1, 2) time(s), yo, k2tog, k2. Knit 2 more rows. Bind off.

SLEEVE

First lay out the Front and Back as in diagram. Then bring the Garter stitch edge at top of Front over Back in such a way that the distance from A to B measures 8 (10, 11, 13) inches. There should be enough overlap for buttons. Tack these pieces in place with

temporary sts as necessary. Then, with RS facing, pick up and k20 (25, 28, 32) sts between B and shoulder (going through both layers of fabric where Front and Back are overlapped); pick up and k21 (26, 29, 33) sts between shoulder and A. There are 41 (51, 57, 65) sts. Remove temporary sts. Purl the next row, and then work Row 1 of sleeve pattern. Continue in patt until sleeve measures 2 inches. Then dec at beginning and end of row every ¾ (¾, 1, 1) inch 5 (6, 6, 7) times, keeping in patt. There are 31 (39, 45, 51) sts. Work until entire sleeve measures 6 (7½, 9, 10½) inches, or ¾ inch less than desired length, ending with a RS row. Knit the following row, dec 5 (8, 8, 10) sts evenly across row. Knit 5 (5, 7, 7) more rows in Garter stitch. Bind off. Work second sleeve in the same manner.

FINISHING

Being careful to make a square corner, sew about 2 inches of upper sleeve edge to cast off sts at bottom of the armhole. Sew side and underarm seams. Sew on buttons. Weave in loose ends.

For washing instructions read "Caring for Handknits" on page xiv.

BABY BONNET

(Pictured in Unbleached White Cotton Comfort on page 76)

Simply perfect for your first child or grand-child, or perhaps destined to become your signature baby gift or donation to a community raffle. The all-over brocade pattern grants this simple cap heirloom status. Sized just right for a carry-along project. Knit one, or one in every color, with or without a ruffle.

An intermediate pattern.

SIZES
Up to 6 mo (6–12 mo, 12–18 mo)

GAUGE
20 sts = 4" (10 cm) in Pattern Stitch

MATERIALS
Yarn
Cotton Comfort, Sylvan Spirit, Granite State Green, or Alpaca Elegance: 1 2 oz skein, all sizes
Needles: Size 6 (4.0 mm) straight or 16" (40 cm) circular, or size required to obtain gauge
Crochet hook: Size C

PATTERN STITCH (SEE CHART)

CAST ON 63 (69, 75) sts. Work in Garter stitch (knit each row) for 10 (12, 12) rows. There will be 5 (6, 6) ridges on each side of work. Then work in PS, repeating the 6 rows until piece measures 4½ (5¼, 6) inches. On the following row, dec 0 (6, 5) st(s) evenly across row. There are 63 (63, 70) sts remaining. Continue decreasing as follows:

Row 1: *K5, k2tog, repeat from *.
Row 2 and all even-numbered rows: Knit all sts.
Row 3: *K4, k2tog, repeat from *.
Row 5: *K3, k2tog, repeat from *.
Row 7: *K2, k2tog, repeat from *.
Row 9: *K1, k2tog, repeat from *.
Row 11: *K2tog, repeat from *.

Break yarn, leaving a 10-inch end. Add the ruffle before sewing up back. To finish hat without a ruffle, thread yarn through remaining sts and pull together firmly. Beginning at this point, sew bonnet together for 3 (3½, 3½) inches. Weave end in on WS of work.

RUFFLE (OPTIONAL)

With RS of work facing, pick up and k62 (67, 72) sts along 4th (5th, 5th) Garter stitch ridge. Knit 1 row. Work an inc row as follows: Knit 1, *inc 1 st in each of the next 4 sts, k1, repeat from *, end with k1. There are 110 (119, 128) sts.

Size 6 months only: Knit 2 more rows. Bind off all sts.

Sizes 6–12 (12–18) months: Knit 1 row. Work another inc row as follows: *Knit 3, inc 1 st in next st, repeat from *; end row with k3 (4). Knit 2 (3) more rows. Bind off all sts.

KEY TO CHART

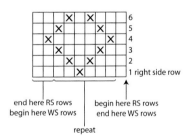

☒ purl on right side rows, knit on wrong side rows

end here RS rows
begin here WS rows

begin here RS rows
end here WS rows

repeat

FINISHING

Weave in loose ends on WS. Work the first tie by crocheting a chain 7 (8, 8) inches long; continue working in sc along bottom edge of bonnet; work second tie by continuing to chain for 7 (8, 8) inches. Break yarn and weave in ends.

For washing instructions read "Caring for Handknits" on page xiv.

Welt Cap, Classy Cap
& Mittens

CLASSY CAP

(Pictured in Coral Bell Mountain Mohair)

To learn or teach knitting in the round, start with the Classy Cap. This cozy cap is knit on circular needles with a double strand of yarn. Choose a rolled or crocheted edge.

An easy pattern.

SIZES
Small (Medium, Large)

FINISHED MEASUREMENTS
Circumference: 20½ (22 ¼, 23)" / 52 (56.5, 58.5) cm

GAUGE
13 sts = 4" (10 cm)

MATERIALS
Yarn
Mountain Mohair or Green Mountain Green: 2 2-oz skeins
Needles: Size 10 (6.0 mm) 24" (60 cm) circular; Size 10 (6.0 mm) dpn, or size required to obtain gauge; tapestry needle
Crochet hook: Size G

CAST ON 67 (72, 75) sts using circular needle and a double strand of yarn. Join, making sure sts are not twisted on needle. Knit until work measures 4 to 5 inches—4½ to 4¾ inches will fit an average adult. (For a rolled-edge finish, knit 1 extra inch.) For sizes Sm and Lg only, dec 3 sts evenly across next round, leaving 64 and 72 sts on needle. Place marker to make decreasing easier.

Decrease as follows (changing to dpn when necessary):
Round 1: *K6, k2tog, repeat from * to end of round.

Round 2 and all even-numbered rounds: Knit all sts.
Round 3: *K5, k2tog, repeat from * to end of round.
Round 5: *K4, k2tog, repeat from * to end of round.
Round 7: *K3, k2tog, repeat from * to end of round.
Round 9: *K2, k2tog, repeat from * to end of round.
Round 11: *K1, k2tog, repeat from * to end of round.
Round 13: K2tog all around.

FINISHING

Break the yarn, leaving at least a 15-inch tail. Using a tapestry needle, thread yarn through rem sts. Pull yarn firm; weave in on WS of work, and then bring yarn to outside through the small hole at top of hat and use it to crochet a 2-inch chain. Make a small pom-pom or tassel and attach to chain. The cap may be finished in two ways. For a crisper edge that won't roll, work 2 rounds of sc around the hem of cap. For a rolled edge, do nothing: The edge will curl up attractively on its own.

For washing instructions read "Caring for Handknits" on page xiv.

"Hats and mittens" conjures up all sorts of memories: receiving them as gifts or the fun of making them yourself and then giving them away. These basic instructions sized for children and adults are the perfect templates for your own creative work. Knit them in your favorite solid color or incorporate colors from your yarn stash to design "a pattern as you go." Enjoy your memories of mittens and create some new ones.

WELT CAP

(Pictured in Peacock, Day Lily, and Coral Bell Mountain Mohair on page 80)

Spinnery friend Candace Brown loves to experiment with bold colors in unexpected combinations. She designed this cap for her grandchild to shake up the color boundaries of Mountain Mohair. Start fresh with new skeins or combine colors from your favorite past projects into one glorious new colorway.

An easy pattern.

SIZES
Child: 2–4 (6–8). **Adult:** Small (Medium, Large).

FINISHED MEASUREMENTS
Circumference: Child: 18 (19)"/45.5 (48.5) cm.
Adult: 20 (21, 22)"/51 (53.5, 56) cm.

GAUGE
16 sts & 20 rows = 4" (10 cm)

MATERIALS
Yarn
Mountain Mohair or Green Mountain Green
Main Color (MC): 1 2 oz skein
Colors A and B: 1 2 oz skein each
Needles: Size 8 (5.0 mm) 16" (40 cm) circular
  and dpn, or size required to obtain gauge

CAST ON 72 (76); 80 (84, 88) sts with MC, using circular needle. Join sts, making sure sts are not twisted on needle. Place marker on needle and knit 1 round with MC. Continue in Color A, knit 1 round, purl 2 rounds. This completes 1 welt. Continue working on the hatband with the following rounds:
*MC: Knit 2 rounds.
Color B: Knit 1 round, p2 rounds.
MC: Knit 2 rounds.
Color A: Knit 1 round, p2 rounds.
Repeat from * 1 more time for Child, 2 more times for Adult.
All sizes: Knit 1 round in MC and then begin dec for top of cap.

FIRST DECREASE ROUND
Sizes 2–4: *K7, k2tog, repeat from * to end of round.
Sizes 6–8: *K8, k2tog, k7, k2tog, repeat from * to end of round.

Size Sm: *K8, k2tog, repeat from * to end of round.
Size Med: *K9, k2tog, k8, k2tog, repeat from * to end of round.
Size Lg: * K9, k2tog, repeat from * to end of round.
All sizes: Knit 2 rounds.

SECOND DECREASE ROUND
Sizes 2–4: *K6, k2tog, repeat from * to end of round.
Sizes 6–8: *K7, k2tog, k6, k2tog, repeat from * to end of round.
Size Sm: *K7, k2tog, repeat from * to end of round.
Size Med: *K8, k2tog, k7, k2tog, repeat from * to end of round.
Size Lg: *K8, k2tog, repeat from * to end of round.
All sizes: Knit 2 rounds.

Continue dec in this manner every 3 rounds. With each succeeding dec round there will be 1 less st before "k2tog." Change to dpn when necessary, and work until 8 sts remain. Knit 2 together around; place all 4 sts on one dpn.

I-CORD TOP KNOT
Using any of the colors, work as follows: *Knit 1 row. Without turning the work, slide sts back to beginning of the row. Pull yarn firmly from end of row. Repeat from *. Work in this manner for 3 inches. Break off a 6-inch tail and draw it through the 4 sts, pulling together firmly. Bring ends to WS.

FINISHING
Weave in loose ends. Tie the I-cord into a knot.

For washing instructions read "Caring for Handknits" on page xiv.

MITTENS

(Pictured in Coral Bell and Peacock Mountain Mohair on page 80)

Warm, long wearing, and comfortably flexible. Spinnery founder Claire Wilson designed this basic pattern and knit the first pair in Mountain Mohair. She wore them daily through five long winters before reknitting the thumbs. Firmly knit on Size 2 double pointed needles. Knit in one color as described in pattern or try some bold experiments as pictured.

An easy pattern.

SIZES
Child: Toddler (Medium, Large)
Adult: Small (Medium, Large)

FINISHED MEASUREMENTS AROUND HAND, ABOVE THUMB OPENING
Child: 5 (5½, 6½)"/12.5 (14, 15) cm
Adult: 8 (9, 10)"/20.5 (23, 25.5) cm

GAUGE
6¼ sts = 1" (2.5 cm)

MATERIALS
Yarn
Double Twist or 2-Ply 100% Wool: 1 4-oz skein, all sizes
Mountain Mohair or Green Mountain Green:
Child: 1 (1, 2) 2 oz skein(s); **Adult:** 2 (2, 2) 2 oz skeins
Needles: Size 2 (2.75 mm) dpn, or size required to obtain gauge; tapestry needle
Stitch holder: 1 small (a large safety pin will do)

CAST ON 33 (36, 39) sts for Child, 45 (51, 57) sts for Adult. Divide sts onto 3 needles, so that each needle has a number of sts divisible by 3. Join sts, being careful not to twist, and work in k2, p1 rib for 2 (2½, 2½) inches for Child, 3 (3½, 3½) inches for Adult. Change to St st and work 3 more rounds for Child, 5 more rounds for Adult.

Thumb gusset for all sizes: Knit 1 st, pm on needle, inc 1 st in each of next 2 sts, pm on needle, knit to end of round. Work next round plain. Continue to inc for gusset every other row by increasing in the st *after* first marker and also in the st *before* second marker. After a total of 5 (5, 6) inc rounds for Child, 8 (10, 11) inc rounds for Adult, work 2 (3, 4) rounds plain for Child, 4 (6, 6) rounds plain for Adult. There are a total of 43 (46, 51) sts for Child, 61 (71, 79) sts for Adult. In the following round, place the

12 (12, 14) thumb sts for Child, 18 (22, 24) thumb sts for Adult, on holder, and cast on 3 (4, 5) sts for Child, 4 (5, 6) sts for Adult. There are a total of 38 (42, 46) sts for Child, 51 (58, 65) sts for Adult. Work straight on these sts until mitten measures 3 (3¾, 4½) inches from ribbing, or ¾ inch less than desired length for Child, and 5½ (6, 6½) inches, or 1½ inches less than desired finished length for Adult.

Decrease for Child (All Sizes)
Round 1: *K2, k2tog, repeat from *.
Rounds 2 & 3: Knit all sts.
Round 4: *K1, k2tog, repeat from *.
Round 5: Knit all sts.
Round 6: *K2 tog, repeat from *.
Break yarn, leaving about 6 inches; thread a tapestry needle with this end and draw yarn through sts, pulling the sts together firmly.

Decrease for Adult (All Sizes)
Round 1: *K5, k2tog, repeat from *.
Rounds 2 & 3: Knit all sts.
Round 4: *K4, k2tog, repeat from *.
Round 5 & 6: Knit all sts.
Round 7: *K3, k2tog, repeat from *.
Rounds 8 & 9: Knit all sts.
Round 10: *K2, k2tog, repeat from *.
Round 11: Knit all sts.
Round 12: *K1, k2tog, repeat from *.
Round 13: * K2 tog, repeat from *.
Break yarn, leaving about 6 inches; thread a tapestry needle with this end and draw yarn through sts, pulling the sts together firmly.

Thumb: Divide sts from holder onto 2 needles. With third needle, pick up 1 st at side of thumb hole; pick up 2 (4, 4) sts at top of hole for Child, 4 (5, 6) sts at top of hole for Adult, and 1 st at other side of hole. On first round, knit together the first 2 sts on third needle, and last 2 sts on third needle. There are a total of 12 (14, 16) sts for Child, 20 (25, 28) sts for Adult. Work straight on these sts until thumb measures 1 (1¼, 1¾) inches for Child, 1¼ (1¼, 1½) inches for Adult.

Decrease for Child: When thumb measures 1 (1¼, 1¾) inches or desired length, *k2tog, repeat from *; break yarn and finish as for top of mitten.

Decrease for Adult: When thumb measures 1¼ (1¼, 1½) inches or ¾ inch less than desired length, work as follows.

Small & Medium: *K3, k2tog, repeat from *; work 2 rows straight.

Large: Work 3 rows straight.

Then, for all sizes:
Round 1: *K2, k2tog, repeat from *.
Round 2 & 3: Knit all sts.
Round 4: *K1, k2tog, repeat from *.
Round 5: *K2tog, repeat from *.
Break yarn and finish as for top of mitten.

Work second mitten the same as the first, except for placement of thumb gusset. To begin gusset, after completing ribbing and 3 rounds of St st for Child, or 5 rounds of St st for Adult, work to within 3 sts of end of round. Place marker on needle, inc 1 st in each end of the next 2 sts, pm on needle, knit last st. Continue inc for gusset in same manner as for first mitten.

FINISHING
Weave in all loose ends on inside of mitten.

For washing instructions read "Caring for Handknits" on page xiv.

Necessary Accessories—*Old and new, tried and true, these five designs cover the bases for cold-weather style and comfort. Suited for every knitting level in many Spinnery yarns.*

Charlotte's Scarf, Eric's Glovelets,
Cynthia's Smorgasbord Socks,
IBH's Toasty Socks &
Maureen's Socks

CHARLOTTE'S SCARF

(Pictured in Sylvan Spirit Luminosity on page 85)

Whether you're strutting down city streets or swinging along a breezy lakeshore path, you'll be stylish and warm in this open-work scarf designed by Charlotte Quiggle. Knit horizontally, the scarf features a pattern stitch that is identical on both sides, and neatly framed by Garter Stitch borders.

An intermediate pattern.

SIZES
One size suits all

FINISHED MEASUREMENTS
Approximately 7" x 64" (18 cm x 163 cm)

GAUGE
15 sts & 36 rows = 4" (10 cm) over PS blocked. It is not critical to achieve an exact gauge for this project.

MATERIALS
Yarn
Sylvan Spirit, Alpaca Elegance, or Cotton Comfort: 3 2 oz skeins
Several yards of waste yarn, same weight as project yarn, for Provisional Cast On
Needle: Size 7 (4.5 mm) 29/36" (80 cm) circular or size needed to obtain gauge
Crochet hook: Size H

PATTERN STITCH
Row 1: Knit 3, *yo, k1; rep from * to last 3 sts, k3.
Row 2: Knit 3, purl to last 3 sts, k3.
Row 3: Knit 3, * k2tog across to last 3 sts, k3.
Rows 4 & 5: Knit 3, *yo, k2tog, rep from * to last 3 sts, k3.
Rows 6 & 7: Knit.

CAST ON 240 sts using your Provisional Cast On yarn of choice. We recommend a crochet cast-on method as follows:

Crochet Cast On: Loosely crochet a chain of at least 240 sts. Use waste yarn about the same weight as your project yarn and a crochet hook a few sizes larger than the knitting needles you will use to work the scarf. Fasten off and tie several knots in the yarn at the end of the chain. With your knitting needles and project yarn, pick up 240 sts in the bumps at the back of the crochet chain. *NB: This cast on is useful when you wish to have loops available at the bottom of the fabric so that you can work down from the edge. You will find it handy when you are unsure exactly how you want to work your border. Binding off the loops gives the fabric identical top and bottom edges.*

Knit 5 rows. Repeat Rows 1–7 of PS 8 times, and then work Rows 1–3 of PS. Knit 5 rows. Bind off very loosely (if necessary, go up 2 needle sizes) in knit. To finish the cast on border, you will need to "free" the loops from the crocheted chain. Beginning at the knotted end of the chain, undo a st and pull, putting each freed-up loop on your needle as you "unzip" the chain. Bind off very loosely in knit.

FINISHING
Weave in ends. To open up the stitches, "wet-blocking" is recommended. Simply roll the scarf into a very damp bath towel, place in a large plastic bag until the scarf is thoroughly damp, and then pin the scarf onto a blocking board until dry.

For washing instructions read "Caring for Handknits" on page xiv.

ERIC'S GLOVELETS

(Pictured in Luminosity Sylvan Spirit on page 85)

Local designer and musician Eric Robinson created these whimsical and functional quick-to-knit wrist warmers to wear in her chilly piano room—necessity was the mother of invention. Now you can have warm hands and a warm heart while you work or play.

An intermediate pattern.

SIZE
Adult Medium

GAUGE
5½ sts = 1" (2.5 cm) in Reverse St stitch

MATERIALS
Yarn
Sylvan Spirit or Cotton Comfort: 1 2 oz skein
Needles: Size 3 (3.25 mm) dpn, or size needed to obtain gauge
Stitch holders: 1 small

PATTERN STITCH
Baby Cable Ribbing (from Barbara G. Walker's *A Treasury of Knitting Patterns*).
Rounds 1, 2 & 3: *P2, k2 repeat from *.
Round 4: *P2, k2tog, but leave on needle; then insert rh needle between the 2 stitches just knitted together, and knit the first st again; then sl both sts from needle together; rep. from *. Repeat Rounds 1–4.

RIGHT GLOVE
CAST ON 48 sts. Divide evenly onto 3 needles and join, being careful not to twist. Work Baby Cable Ribbing for approximately 3½ inches, ending with Round 1. Next round: P1, pm on needle, p1, k2, p1, pm on needle, work 17 sts in Reverse St stitch (purl all sts), continue in patt to end of round. (The 4 sts between the markers will become the thumb gusset.) Continue in this manner for 3 more rounds.

Next round: P1, slip marker, p1, m1 right, k2, m1 left, p1, continue as established.

Continue working thumb gusset, Reverse St stitch, and Baby Cable Ribbing, making increases after the first purl st and before the last purl st of thumb gusset every third round, until there are 16 sts between the markers for the thumb.

On next round, slip 16 thumb sts onto a holder or piece of yarn. Cast on 5 sts. Purl the next st and pass the fifth cast on st over, and then continue around hand as established (48 sts). Work the cast on sts in Reverse St stitch.

On next Round 1 of Baby Cable Ribbing, work the pattern on all sts. Complete Rounds 2–4, then repeat Rounds 1 & 2.

On next round, bind off in patt.

Transfer thumb sts from holder to 2 needles. Leaving a 6-inch tail, work these sts, continuing the Baby Cable Ribbing. Pick up and knit 5 sts on top of thumb opening. Purl the next st and pass the last picked up st over (20 sts). Work these thumb sts for one completion of the pattern, then repeat Rounds 1 & 2. Bind off on next round.

LEFT GLOVE
Work cuff as for Right Glove, beginning Baby Cable Ribbing with k2 instead of p2. Next round: K2 (p2, k2) 6 times, p17, pm on needle for thumb gusset, p1, k2, p1, pm on needle, p1.

Work 3 more rounds as established: 26 sts in patt for the back of the hand, 17 sts in Reverse St stitch, and the thumb gusset, end p1. Continue as for Right Glove, with reversed shaping.

FINISHING
Weave in loose ends.

For washing instructions read "Caring for Handknits" on page xiv.

CYNTHIA'S SMORGASBORD SOCKS

(Pictured in Edelweiss Mountain Mohair on page 85)

Cynthia Wise designed these basic socks to feature lots of texture: Seed Stitch, Double Seed Stitch, Garter Stitch, and Reverse Stockinette Stitch. For added interest, work each section in a different color.

An easy pattern.

SIZES
Adult: Small (Medium, Large)

FINISHED MEASUREMENTS
Heel to toe: approx 8¼ (9, 10½)" / 21 (23, 26.5) cm

GAUGE
5 sts = 2.5 cm in St st

MATERIALS
Yarn: Mountain Mohair 2 (2, 3) 2 oz skeins
Needles: Size 5 (3.75 mm) dpn

CAST ON 44 sts. Divide sts onto 3 needles. This is Round 1. Join work, making sure sts are not twisted on the needles, and work cuff as follows:
Rounds 2 & 3: Purl.
Round 4: Knit.
Rounds 5–14: *K2, p2, repeat from * to end of round.
Round 15: Knit.
Rounds 16 & 17: Purl.
Round 18: Knit.
Rounds 19 & 21: *K1, p1, repeat from * to end of round.
Round 20: *P1, k1, repeat from * to end of round.
Rounds 22 & 23: Knit.
Rounds 24 & 25: Purl.
Round 26: Knit.
Rounds 27, 28, 31, 32, 35, 36: *K2, p2, repeat from * to end of round.
Rounds 29, 30, 33, 34, 37, 38: *P2, k2, repeat from * to end of round.
Round 39: Knit.

Rounds 40 & 41: Purl.
Rounds 42, 43, 44: Knit.
Round 45: Purl.
Rounds 46 & 47: Knit.
Round 48: Purl.
Rounds 49 & 50: Knit.
Round 51: Purl.
Round 52: Knit.
Rounds 53 & 55: *Knit 1, p1, repeat from * to end of round.
Round 54: *Purl 1, k1, repeat from * to end of round.
Rounds 56 & 59: Knit.
Rounds 57 & 58: Purl.
This completes the cuff.

HEEL

Break yarn, leaving approx 4 inches. Arrange sts for the heel as follows: Transfer 10 sts from first needle and 10 sts from third needle onto 1 needle for back of heel. Leaving 12 sts on each of the other 2 needles, work back and forth on the 20 heel sts in St st, slipping the first st of each row. Work 20 rows; there will be 10 slipped sts on each side of this section.

HEEL CAP

Slip first st wyib, k13, ssk, turn. *Slip first st wyif, p8, p2tog, turn. Slip first st wyib, k8, ssk, turn. Repeat from * until 10 sts remain.

INSTEP

Knit the 10 sts of heel cap; these sts are on Needle #1. Still using Needle #1, pick up and k1 st in each of the 10 slipped sts. Using Needle #2, knit the next 24 sts. With Needle #3, pick up and knit 1 st in each of the remaining slipped sts. Knit 5 sts of heel cap and transfer them to Needle #3. This completes Round 1. Decrease as follows every third round:
Needle #1: Knit to last 2 sts, k2tog.
Needle #2: Knit all sts.
Needle #3: Slip 2 sts, one at a time, as if to knit; insert left needle into front of sts

and k2tog (left-slanted decrease); knit remaining sts.

Decrease in this manner 7 times. There are 40 sts remaining.

FOOT
Work next 4 rounds as follows:
Rounds 1 & 3: *K1, p1, repeat from * to end of round.
Rounds 2 & 4: *P1, k1, repeat from * to end of round.
Knit straight until foot portion of sock reaches the base of your little toe, or 7 (14, 27) more rounds. Work Rounds 1 through 4 as above.

TOE
*K4, k2tog, repeat from *, knit last 4 sts.
Knit 4 rounds.
*K3, k2tog, repeat from *, end round with k2, k2tog.
Knit 3 rounds.
*K2, k2tog, repeat from *, knit last 3 sts.
Knit 2 rounds.
*K1, k2tog, repeat from * to end of round.
Knit 1 round.
*K2 tog, repeat from * to end of round.

There are 7 sts remaining. Draw yarn through these sts and pull firmly. Make second sock to match.

FINISHING
Weave in loose ends.

For washing instructions read "Caring for Handknits" on page xiv.

IBH's Toasty Socks

(Pictured in Vermont Organic 100% Wool on page 85)

Idabelle Hegemann had twenty-six grand-children and great-grandchildren and knit socks for each of them annually. Her step-by-step teaching pattern will have you confidently knitting a rib pattern in the round, turning a heel, and finishing the toe with Kitchener Stitch. Custom-fit these sturdy boot socks by changing needle size and adjusting the length of cuff and foot. Toasty Socks is the first printed Spinnery pattern, a gift from Mrs. Hegemann on the occasion of the spinnery's founding in December 1981.

An easy pattern.

SIZE
Adult Medium

GAUGE
6 sts = 1" (2.5 cm) in in St st

MATERIALS
Yarn
Double Twist or 2-Ply Wool, Mountain Mohair, Green Mountain Green, or Vermont Organic
Main Color (MC): 4 oz
Darker Color (DC): 40 yds, approx1 oz
Lighter Color (LC): 40 yds, approx1 oz
Needles: Size 3 (3.25mm) dpn or size needed to obtain gauge; tapestry needle

---

CAST ON 48 sts in DC. Divide the sts, 16 on each of 3 needles, and join, being careful not to twist. Work in k2, p2 ribbing for 7 rows. Works stripes in ribbing as follows: 2 rows LC; 2 rows DC; 4 rows LC; 2 rows DC; 2 rows LC.

Finish the ribbing with 7 rows of DC.

Change to MC and k6, p2 around row. Continue in k6, p2 ribbing until sock measures 12 inches, or desired length to top of heel. Place half the sts (24) on one needle (the heel needle) so that the pattern is k3, p2, k6, p2, k6, p2, k3.

HEEL
With DC, work as follows:
Row 1 with WS facing: * Slip 1, p1, repeat from * across heel needle.
Row 2: Slip first st, knit all other sts.
Repeat these 2 rows until heel measures 2½ inches.

TURNING THE HEEL
Using MC, with WS facing:
Row 1: S1, p11, p2tog, p1, turn.
Row 2: S1, k2, k2tog, k1, turn.
Row 3: S1, p3, p2tog, p1, turn.
Row 4: S1, k4, k2tog, k1, turn.
Row 5: S1, p5, p2tog, p1, turn.
Row 6: S1, k6, k2tog, k1, turn.

Row 7: S1, p7, p2tog, p1, turn.
Row 8: S1, k8, k2tog, k1, turn.
Row 9: S1, p9, p2tog, p1, turn.
Row 10: S1, k10, k2tog, k1, turn.
Row 11: S1, p11, p2tog, p1, turn.
Row 12: S1, k10, k2tog, k1, turn.
Twelve sts remain.

INSTEP AND FOOT
Using MC and with RS facing, with the heel needle pick up and k13 sts on left edge of heel. Work across instep, following Rib Pattern (k3, p2, k6, p2, k6, p2, k3).

With fourth needle, pick up and k13 sts on other edge of heel, and with the same needle, knit the first 6 sts from the heel needle. Now place all the sts for instep on one needle. The sts are distributed as follows:

Needle A: From the middle of heel up side of heel (19 sts).

Needle B: Instep (24 sts).

Needle C: Down other side to middle of heel (19 sts).

Decrease:

Row 1: Knit sts on A, work in ribbing on B, knit sts on C.

Row 2: On A, knit to within 3 sts of end, k2tog, k1 on B, work across in Rib Pattern on C, k1, sl 1, k1, psso, knit to end.

Repeat these 2 rows until 11 sts remain on Needles A and C. Continue to work with no more dec until foot measures 5½ inches from center back of heel. Then, on B, k2tog in the first and third purl ribs, leaving 22 sts on needle.

Work for 2 more inches. Then knit all of the 22 sts on B, ending with the purl rib.

Continue knitting to within 2½ inches of desired length of sock. Knit 5 rows in DC; knit 3 rows in LC.

TOE

Change to DC and begin decreases.

Needle A: Knit to within 3 sts of end, k2tog, k1.

Needle B: K1, sl 1, k1, psso, knit to within 3 sts of end, k2tog, k1.

Needle C: K1, sl 1, k1, psso, knit to end.

Continue to dec in this manner each row until 12 sts remain. Knit sts from Needle A and then move them to Needle C. There are now 2 needles, each having 6 sts. Break yarn, leaving about 12 inches, and thread the yarn in a tapestry needle. Hold the knitting needles parallel to each other, with yarn at the right end of back needle.

Bind off using Kitchener Stitch as described in "Using the Patterns" on page xiv.

Make a second sock to match.

FINISHING

Weave in all ends.

For washing instructions read "Caring for Handknits" on page xiv.

MAUREEN'S SOCKS

(Pictured in Silver Cotton Comfort on page 85)

Maureen Clark worked a variation on Barbara G. Walker's Pagoda Lace Pattern to create this airy, all-season sock. Designed for our Cotton Comfort blend, the sock features yarn over stitches along the instep and a Picot edge cuff.

An intermediate pattern.

SIZES
Adult Small, Medium, Large

FINISHED MEASUREMENTS
Heel to toe: Approx 9 (9½, 10½)"/23 (24, 26.5) cm
Cuff to below ankle: Approx 6"/15 cm

GAUGE
24 sts = 4" (10 cm) in St st

MATERIALS
Yarn
Cotton Comfort: 2 2 oz skeins
Needles: Size 3 (3.25 mm) dpn; tapestry needle

CUFF
CAST ON 48 sts. Arrange sts as follows: Needle #1, 23 sts; Needle #2, 12 sts; Needle #3, 13 sts. Join, making sure sts are not twisted on the needles. Knit 8 rounds. The following round is a Picot round: *k2 tog, yo, repeat from * to end of round. Then knit 8 more rounds.

LEG
Work Lace Panel Pattern from chart on Needle #1; knit all sts on Needles #2 & #3. Work approx 5½ inches of Lace Panel Pattern, or desired length to heel. Rearrange the sts so that the Lace stitches are on 2 needles and the rem 25 sts are on one needle for the heel.

HEEL
Work short rows back and forth on the heel needle, i.e., work 1 less st in each succeeding row.

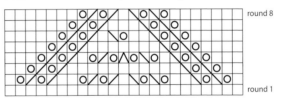

LACE PANEL PATTERN for small, medium & ex-large

round 8

round 1

KEY TO CHART
☐ knit
⊙ yo
╱ k2 tog
╲ ssk
⋀ k3 tog

Short Rows
Row 1: S1, p22, turn.
Row 2: S1, k21, turn.
Row 3: S1, p20, turn.
Row 4: Sl1, k19, turn.
Continue in this manner.
Row 17: S1, p6, turn.
Row 18: S1, k6, turn.
Now work 1 more st in each row.
Row 19: S1, p7, turn.
Row 20: S1, k8, turn.
Continue in this way.
Row 33: S1, p21, turn.
Row 34 (last heel row): S1, k23.

FOOT
Rearrange the sts as they were before the heel, working Lace Panel Pattern on Needle #1 and St st on the rem 25 sts divided between Needles #2 & #3. Continue working until foot is 1½ inches less than desired length.

TOE (WORKED IN ST ST)
Round 1
Needle #1: K1, ssk, knit to last 3 sts, k2tog, k1.
Needle #2: K1, ssk, knit to end.
Needle #3: Knit to last 3 sts, k2tog, k1.

Round 2: Knit all sts.

Alternate these 2 rounds until 28 sts remain. On the following round, decrease only on Needles #2 & #3.

Then *k2tog, k2tog, k2tog, k1, k2tog, k2tog, k2tog, repeat from *. Transfer the sts from Needle #3 to Needle #2.

There are 7 sts on each needle. Hold needles parallel to each other, with yarn at the right end of the back needle.

Bind off using Kitchener Stitch as described in "Using the Patterns" on page xiv.

Make second sock same as the first.

FINISHING

Turn cuff on Picot round and tack in place. Weave in loose ends.

For washing instructions read "Caring for Handknits" on page xiv.

APPENDIXES

What Makes Spinnery Yarns So Special?

The design of our yarns is inspired by the natural fibers themselves. Every step in the process of turning fibers into yarn is monitored carefully by our experienced team, from sorting, scouring, picking, carding, and spinning to the final finishing. Here is how we turn natural fibers into yarns of beauty and distinction.

Sorting

Selection of high-quality fibers is the first step toward creating a great yarn. All raw fibers—wool, mohair, alpaca, and organic cotton—are evaluated and sorted by hand for color, softness, luster, crimp, resilience, and length. Each wool type has its own virtues: e.g., Romney is known for length and luster; Corriedale for crimp; Merino, Targhee, and Rambouillet for fineness. For our 100% New England wool yarns we look for fleece that will give texture, softness, and strength, while our Mountain Mohair and Cotton Comfort need blends of the silkier and finer fibers. Once fibers have been selected and sorted they are ready for scouring.

Scouring

Raw fleece and fibers are washed. Our *GREENSPUN* scouring system is designed to conserve and recycle water. A hot-water soak breaks down the fleece's lanolin and removes dirt. We use soda ash and biodegradable vegetable-based soap for washing.

Once clean, the fibers are rinsed and dried, ready for picking.

Picking

To create a particular yarn, scoured locks of different types are mixed together and "fluffed" to separate the individual fibers. Each type of wool has its own virtues. The correct proportions of different fiber types and colors—dyed and/or natural—are weighed and layered by hand. Fibers are misted with light oil to reduce static and prepare them for carding. A vegetable-based oil is used on the *GREENSPUN* fibers, and a commercial spinning oil is used for all other yarn lines.

Carding

As picked wool passes over carding cylinders the fibers are blended, brushed, and trans-formed into pencil rovings. Picked fiber is loaded into the hopper of our carding machine. Settings are adjusted to match the specific requirements of each fiber mix: Longer, slippery fibers like Romney and Churro move more quickly through the machine than finer wools, such as Merino and Targhee. The carding process creates a gossamer sheet of fiber, which is then divided into individual strands called pencil rovings and wound onto spools ready for spinning.

Spinning

Carded pencil rovings are now twisted in the spinning process. Our spinning frame provides endless opportunities for yarn design. Spools of pencil rovings are placed on the spinning frame and are threaded, as required for each particular yarn. For example, Mountain Mohair is created from three strands of roving, combined into a single yarn, while Cotton Comfort is spun from single strands of roving which are then plied. As the carded wool is spun into yarn, it is wound onto bobbins, ready for the final steps of finishing.

Finishing

After spinning, new yarn is steamed and prepared for sale. Steaming the fresh yarn on bobbins sets its twist. Next, yarn is wound onto cones or into skeins, which are individually inspected, weighed, and labeled by hand. Mountain Mohair, Alpaca Elegance, and Green Mountain Green are hand-washed for loft and softness.

Now the yarns are ready for your hands and your inspiration.

YARNS FOR KNITTING AND WEAVING

OUR *GREENSPUN* COLLECTION

If environmental concerns are foremost in your heart, explore our *GREENSPUN* collection in a range of natural colors. These luxury blends of wool with alpaca, mohair, and organic cotton are processed using our innovative and environmentally sound methods. Fibers for *GREENSPUN* yarns are washed and spun with vegetable-based soaps and oils rather than the petroleum-based products standard in the textile industry. No chemicals are used to bleach, shrink-proof, or moth-proof. The *GREENSPUN* process, developed at the Spinnery, is an extension of the environmental concerns basic to our founding in 1981.

GREEN MOUNTAIN GREEN

Our softest, most luxurious yarn. We combine the best kid mohair with the finest wool in natural colors to produce a range of subtle hues. Exquisitely soft and lofty, Green Mountain Green will provide you with hours of knitting and wearing pleasure.

60% Fine Wool / 40% Kid Mohair, 2-ply worsted weight
Skein: 2 oz / Approx 125 yds (57 g/153 m)
Sts / inch: 3½ to 5
Needles: 5 to 10½ (3.75 to 6.5 mm)
Sett: 8 epi

white
variegated
silver brown

ALPACA ELEGANCE

Wonderful in hand, this yarn showcases the drape and resilience of New England alpaca, the elasticity of fine wool, and the softness of both. *GREENSPUN* in four natural colors.

50% Fine Wool / 50% Alpaca, 2-ply DK weight
Skein: 2 oz / Approx 180 yds (57 g/197 m)
Sts / inch: 5 to 6
Needles: 5 to 7 (3.75 to 4.5 mm)
Sett: 8 to 10 epi

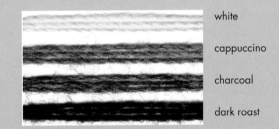

white
cappuccino
charcoal
dark roast

COTTON COMFORT

All the virtues of our dyed Cotton Comfort, but *GREENSPUN* in two natural colors: Unbleached White and Silver.

80% Fine Wool / 20% Organic Cotton, 2-ply DK weight
Skein: 2 oz / Approx 180 yds (57 g/197 m)
Cones: 8 oz / 720 yds (228 g/788 m)
Sts / inch: 5 to 7½
Needles: 1 to 6 (2.25 to 4 mm)
Sett: 8 to 10 epi

6-uw

6-s

unbleached white
silver

GRANITE STATE GREEN

Fine wool from sheep grazing the transmission line rights-of-way in New Hampshire is spun into yarn using our *GREENSPUN* method. Controlling vegetation in this quiet, pastoral way reduces the use of herbicides and petroleum-powered machinery. Perfect for delicate garments and shawls.

100% Fine Wool 2-ply DK weight
Skein: 2 oz / Approx. 180 yds (57 g/197 m)
Sts / Inch: 5 to 6
Needles: 4 to 6
 (3.5 to 4 mm)
Sett: 8 to 10 epi

VERMONT ORGANIC

We are happy to support Vermont shepherds raising sheep by organic methods. Our *GREENSPUN* processing preserves the natural qualities of the wool, making this yarn a perfect choice for Aran and textured projects. Certified organic wool and processing.

100% Organic Wool, 2-ply worsted weight
Skein: 4 oz / Approx 250 yds (114 g/273 m)
Sts / inch: 4½ to 6
Needles: 3 to 7 (3.25 to 4.5 mm)
Sett: 8 to 10 epi

white

grey

CLASSIC COLLECTION

If color stirs your soul, you'll find yourself gravitating toward Mountain Mohair in its range of thirty vibrant hues. Cotton Comfort offers a choice of softer tones. Or try our sturdy 100 percent New England wool yarn in sixteen natural or classic dyed colors.

MOUNTAIN MOHAIR

Begin with wool that is lustrous, resilient, and fine. Add yearling mohair from angora goats to achieve maximum sheen and softness. This lofty yarn is perfect for almost every knitting project and can be combined with our other worsted-weight yarns in multicolor projects.

70% Fine Wool / 30% Yearling Mohair, worsted weight
Skein: 2 oz / Approx 140 yds (57 g/153 m)
Cones: 8 oz / 560 yds (228 g/613 m)
Sts / inch: 3½ to 6
Needles: 2 to 10½ (2.75 to 6.5 mm)
Sett: 8 epi

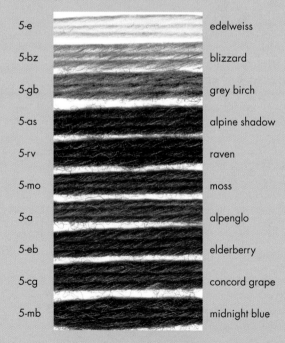

5-e — edelweiss
5-bz — blizzard
5-gb — grey birch
5-as — alpine shadow
5-rv — raven
5-mo — moss
5-a — alpenglo
5-eb — elderberry
5-cg — concord grape
5-mb — midnight blue

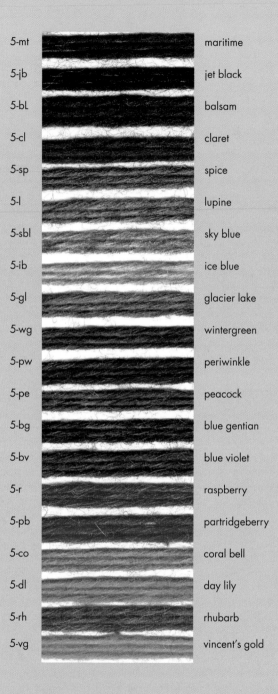

5-mt — maritime
5-jb — jet black
5-bL — balsam
5-cl — claret
5-sp — spice
5-l — lupine
5-sbl — sky blue
5-ib — ice blue
5-gl — glacier lake
5-wg — wintergreen
5-pw — periwinkle
5-pe — peacock
5-bg — blue gentian
5-bv — blue violet
5-r — raspberry
5-pb — partridgeberry
5-co — coral bell
5-dl — day lily
5-rh — rhubarb
5-vg — vincent's gold

COTTON COMFORT

This versatile yarn combines the pure softness of organic cotton with the elasticity and delicacy of fine wool. The knitted fabric is elegant but casual, light but warm, wearable year-round.

80% Fine Wool / 20% Organic Cotton, 2-ply DK weight
Skein: 2 oz / Approx 180 yds (57 g/197 m)
Cones: 8 oz / 720 yds (228 g/788 m)
Sts / inch: 5 to 7½
Needles: 1 to 6 (2.25 to 4 mm)
Sett: 8 to 10 epi

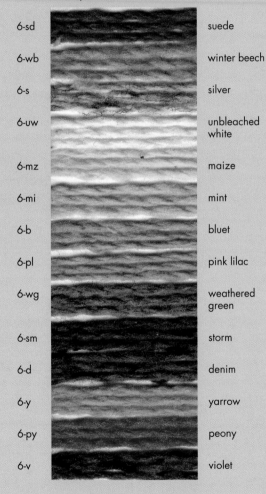

6-sd	suede
6-wb	winter beech
6-s	silver
6-uw	unbleached white
6-mz	maize
6-mi	mint
6-b	bluet
6-pl	pink lilac
6-wg	weathered green
6-sm	storm
6-d	denim
6-y	yarrow
6-py	peony
6-v	violet

SYLVAN SPIRIT

Fine wool and TENCEL® combine to make a soft yarn with a satiny luster and distinctive drape. Lyocel, marketed under the trade name TENCEL® Lyocel, is a cellulosic fiber made from wood pulp, a natural and renewable resource. It is harvested from tree farms exercising responsible forest stewardship and accredited by associations such as the Sustainable Forestry Initiative.

50% Fine Wool / 50% TENCEL® Lyocel DK weight
Skein: 2 oz / Approx. 180 yds (57 g/197 m)
St / inch: 5 to 6
Needles: 4 to 6 (3.5 to 4.0 mm)
Sett: 8 to 10 epi

	luminosity
	moonshadow

2-PLY WOOL AND DOUBLE TWIST

High-quality, medium-grade wools selected from regional farms are blended to create a sturdy, crisp yarn. Combines well with Mountain Mohair.

100% Wool, worsted weight
Skein: 4 oz / Approx 250 yds (114 g / 273 m)
Needles: 3 to 7 (3.25 to 4.5 mm)
Sts / inch: 4½ to 6
Cones: 8 oz / 500 yds (228 g/546 m)
Sett: 8 epi
White and Natural Grey also available as singles sport weight and as Energized Singles.
Cones: 8 oz / 1,000 yds (228 g/1094 m)
Sts/inch: 6
Needles: 4 (3.5 mm)
Sett: 10 to 12 epi

2-Ply Wool

2-w	white
2-ng	natural grey
2-gr	grey ragg
2-ch	chestnut

Double Twist

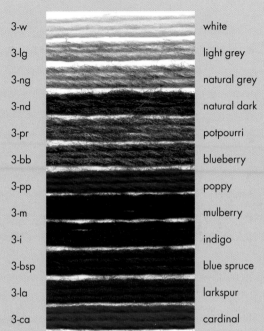

3-w	white
3-lg	light grey
3-ng	natural grey
3-nd	natural dark
3-pr	potpourri
3-bb	blueberry
3-pp	poppy
3-m	mulberry
3-i	indigo
3-bsp	blue spruce
3-la	larkspur
3-ca	cardinal

YARN OVER

Carded wool and mohair left from a range of Spinnery dye lots is blended to create "once only" muted colors in red, blue, green, and gray. Ideal for sturdy sweaters and outerwear.

Wool with some mohair, 2-ply heavy worsted weight
Skein: 4 oz / 155 yds (144 g/185 m)
Sts / inch: 3½ to 4½
Needles: 7 to 10 (4.5 to 6.0 mm)
Sett: 6 to 8 epi

	natural grey
	slate green
	blue
	red

Chart of Patterns

	Pattern	Skill Level	St/in	Needle Size	Finished Measurement (chest/size)	Mountain Mohair (MM) or Green Mountain Green (GMG)	Cotton Comfort (CCM) or Alpaca Elegance (AE)	Sylvan Spirit (SS) or Granite State Green (GSG)	Double Twist or 2-Ply Wool (DT) or Vermont Organic (VO)	Yarn Over
CHILDREN	Easy Raglan (page 12) ★	E	4½	C 5, 7	24, 26, 28, 30, 32	MM: 3, 4, 5, 6, 7 GMG: 4, 5, 6, 7, 8			DT: 2, 2, 3, 3, 4	
	Green Mountain Gardens Cardigan (page 25) ★ ♥	A	5	C 3, 5, 7 dpn 3, 5, 7	30, 33, 35½	MM: Poppies & Pansies: 11, 14, 14 Daisies & Delphiniums: 9, 11, 11 Mosses & Berries: 9, 11, 11 Winter Woods: 10, 13, 13				
	Puntas Sweater ★ ♥ (page 32)	E	4	C 9 dpn 8, 9	24, 26, 28, 30, 32	MM: MC: 4, 4, 4, 5, 6 CC: A & B 1 each				
	Rebecca's Little Sweater (page 77)	I	5	S 6	22¼, 25, 27, 29½		(CCM & AE) 2, 3, 4, 5	GSG: 2, 3, 4, 5		
	Rosemary's Little Sweater (page 23)	E	4	C 8, 9 dpn 8, 9	24, 26, 28, 30, 32	MM: 3, 4, 4, 5, 6				
	Stained Glass Pullover ★ ♥ (page 15)	A	5	C 5, 6, 7 dpn 7	24, 26, 29, 31, 32	MM: Colorway 1: 10, 10, 12, 12, 12 Colorway 2: 8, 8, 9, 9, 10 Colorway 3: 8, 8, 9, 9, 10				
	Stars & Bars Cardigan & Pullover (page 69) ★ ♥	I	5	C 5, 7 dpn 5	24, 26, 28, 30, 32		MC: 3, 4, 4, 5, 5 CC: 1 ea. of 3			
ADULTS	Artisan's Vest (page 3)	E	5	C 5, 6 ch E	36, 40, 44, 48, 52	MM: 4, 6, 7, 7, 8 GMG: 4, 6, 8, 8, 9	3, 4, 5, 5, 6 (CCM & AE)	3, 4, 5, 5, 6 (SS & GSG)	DT: 2, 3, 4, 4, 5	
	Cable Cardigan (page 42)	I	4½	C 8	36, 40, 44, 48, 52	MM: 9, 10, 11, 12, 13 GMG: 10, 12, 13, 14, 15			DT: 5, 6, 7, 7, 8	
	Cable Weave Pullover (page 52)	I	4, 4¾	C or dpn 7	34, 38, 42, 46, 50, 54	MM: 8, 9, 10, 11, 12, 13				
	Candace's Eyelet Sweater (page 37)	A	4	C 7, 9	39, 44, 50, 55	MM: 9, 10, 11, 12 (Long) MM: 7, 8, 9, 10 (Short)				
	Cotton Comfort T-Shirt (page 73)	I	5⅓	S 5, 7, 10 ch C	36, 40, 44, 48, 52		5, 5, 6, 7, 8 (+1 for ¾ sleeve)	SS: 5, 5, 6, 7, 8 (+1 for ¾ sleeve)		
	Cozy Vest (page 8)	E	6½	C 7	35, 39½, 44, 49	MM: 10, 11, 12, 14 GMG: 11, 13, 14, 16			DT: 5, 6, 7, 8	
	Easy Raglan ★ (page 12)	E	4½	C 5, 7 roll and cable neck S 5 cable neck	34, 38, 42, 46, 50, 54	MM: 8, 9, 10, 11, 12, 13 GMG: 9, 11, 12, 13, 14, 15			DT: 5, 5, 6, 7, 7, 7	

Pattern	Skill Level	St/in	Needle Size	Finished Measurement (chest/size)	Mountain Mohair (MM) or Green Mountain Green (GMG)	Cotton Comfort (CCM) or Alpaca Elegance (AE)	Sylvan Spirit (SS) or Granite State Green (GSG)	Double Twist or 2-Ply Wool (DT) or Vermont Organic (VO)	Yarn Over
Energized Vest (page 56)	I	6,7½, 8	C 2, 4, 5 ch E	48				Energized Wool Singles: 2 cones	
Green Mountain Gardens Cardigan (page 25) ★ ♥	A	5	C 3, 5, 7 dpn 3, 5, 7	39¼, 44¾, 50½	MM: Poppies & Pansies: 19, 21, 21 Daisies & Delphiniums: 15, 17, 18 Mosses & Berries: 15, 18, 19 Winter Woods: 18, 19, 21				
Lace Cardigan (page 65)	A	5¾	C 5, S 5	37½, 40½, 44, 47½		6,7,8,9			
Moriah's Wildflower Sweater (page 40)	I	4	S 7, 9	38, 42, 46	MM: 7, 8, 8 GMG: 8, 9, 10				6,6,7
Norwegian Roses Cardigan (page 46) ♥	I	5	C 6,7 S 6 ch E	40, 44, 48, 52	MM: Colorway 1: 11, 13, 14, 16 Colorway 2: 11, 13, 14, 16			DT: Colorway 1: 11, 13, 14, 16 Colorway 2: 11, 13, 14, 16	
Puntas Sweater ★ ♥ (page 32)	E	4	C 9 dpn 8, 9	34, 38, 42, 46, 50	MM: MC: 8, 9, 10, 11,12 CC: A & B: 1 each				
Putney Aran Tunic (page 61)	I	6	C 3, S 3, 5	37, 41, 45, 50, 54		CCM: 8,9,10, 11,12	SS: 8,9,10,11, 12		
Rosemary's Middle-Sized Sweater (page 21)	E	4	C 8, 10 dpn 8	40, 44, 48	MM: 8, 9, 9 GMG: 9, 10, 11				
Spinnery Jacket (page 5)	E	4	S 6, 7 ch G	34, 38, 42, 46, 50, 54	MM: 8,9,11,11,12,13				7, 7, 8, 8, 9, 10
Stained Glass Pullover ★ ♥ (page 15)	A	5	C 5, 6, 7 dpn 7	37, 40, 44, 48, 52			MM: Colorway 1: 15, 18, 24, 24, 24 Colorway 2: 14, 15, 21, 22, 23 Colorway 3: 14, 15, 21, 22, 23		
Stars & Bars Cardigan & Pullover ★ ♥ (page 69)	I	5	C 5, 7 dpn 5	36, 40, 44, 48, 52		MC: 7, 7, 8, 10, 11; CC: 1 each of 3			

(Vertical label at left: ADULTS)

continued on next page

KEY

★ child & adult sizes   ♥ call us for contrasting (CC, DC, LC) color amounts   A: Advanced   C: Circular needles   CC: Contrasting color

ch: Crochet hook   DC: Dark color   dpn: double pointed needles   E: Easy   I: Intermediate   LC: Lighter color   MC: Main color   S: Straight needles

APPENDIXES   101

CHART OF PATTERNS (CONTINUED)

	Pattern	Skill Level	St/in	Needle Size	Finished Measurement (chest/size)	Mountain Mohair (MM) or Green Mountain Green (GMG)	Cotton Comfort (CCM) or Alpaca Elegance (AE)	Sylvan Spirit (SS) or Granite State Green (GSG)	Double Twist or 2-Ply Wool (DT) or Vermont Organic (VO)	Yarn Over
ACCESSORIES	Baby Bonnet (page 79)	I	5	S or C 6, ch C	Up to 6 mo, 6–12 mo, 12–18 mo		CCM: 1, 1, 1 AE: 1, 1	1, 1, 1	1, 1, 1	
	Charlotte's Scarf (page 86)	I	3¾	C 7, ch H	7" x 64"		CCM: 3 AE: 3	SS: 3		
	Classy Cap (page 81)	E	3½	C, dpn 10	Adult: Sm, Med, Lg	MM: 2, 2, 2				
	Cynthia's Smorgasbord Socks (page 88)	E	5	dpn 5	Adult: Sm, Med, Lg	MM: 2, 2, 3				
	Eric's Glovelets (page 87)	I	5½	dpn 3	Adult: Med		CCM: 1	SS: 1		
	IBH's Toasty Socks ♥ (page 90)	E	6	dpn 3	Adult: Med	MC: 2, DC: 1, LC: 1			MC: 1, DC: 1 LC: 1	
	Maureen's Socks (page 92)	I	6	dpn 3	Adult: Sm, Med, Lg		CCM: 2, 2, 2			
	Mittens ★ (page 83)	E	6¼	dpn 2	Child: Toddler, Med, Lg Adult: Sm, Med, Lg	Child: 1, 1, 2 Adult: 2, 2, 2			DT: 1	
	Punta Edged Cap ★ ♥ (page 35)	E	4	C 7 dpn 7	Child: Infant, 2–4, 6–8 yrs Adult: Sm, Med, Lg	MM: MC: 1 CC: 1 each of 2				
	Welt Cap ★ ♥ (page 82)	E	4	C 8 dpn 8	Child: 18, 19 Adult: 20, 21, 22	MC: 2 CC: 1 each of 2				

KEY

★ child & adult sizes   ♥ call us for contrasting (CC, DC, LC) color amounts   A: Advanced   C: Circular needles   CC: Contrasting color
ch: Crochet hook   DC: Dark color   dpn: douple pointed needles   E: Easy   I: Intermediate   LC: Lighter color   MC: Main color   S: Straight needles

FOR A CATALOG, YARN SAMPLES, OR
TO PLACE AN ORDER, CONTACT:

Green Mountain Spinnery
P.O. Box 568
Putney, Vermont 05346
1-800-321-9665 (phone)
802-387-4841 (fax)
spinnery@sover.net
Check www.spinnery.com for the yarn dealer nearest you.

ACKNOWLEDGMENTS

The Green Mountain Spinnery Knitting Book was created at the welcome suggestion of Kermit Hummel and The Countryman Press. Thank you to Kermit, Ann Kraybill, Jennifer Thompson, and Fred Lee, who expertly guided our efforts to bring this book to fruition.

This book could not have been written without the good wishes and generous support of Spinnery founders Libby Mills, David Ritchie, and Claire Wilson, and staff members Margaret Atkinson, Emilie Beauchamp, Maureen Clark, Peter Caouette, Liz Elliott, Dan Harlow, Marshall Gilbert, Jaydl McCaffrey, Eric Robinson, and Laura Simoneau.

My deepest thanks to the following artists, knitters, and friends, who were unstintingly generous in turning their talent, time, and support to creating this book.

Art direction for all photography: Jillfrances Gray

Principal photography: Jeffrey Coolidge

Additional photography: Heidi Wells Photography, Inc., and Kindra Clineff (page x)

Technical and pattern editing: Charlotte Quiggle

Schematics and chart graphics: Joy Wallens-Penford

Copyediting: Hilly Van Loon

Model knitters: Kathe Amaio, Margaret Atkinson, Maureen Clark, Amy Detjen, Susan Florey, Linda Gordon, Melissa Lumley, Libby Mills, Lisa Lloyd, Susan Miles, Charlotte Quiggle, Rita Reilly, Judith "Eric" Robinson, Marty Spencer, and Claire Wilson.

Properties: Jeffrey and Ellen Coolidge, Ian and Jenny Eddy, Jillfrances Gray, Melissa Lumley, Libby Mills, David Tansey, and Scott Farm. My thanks to Andrea and Tom Colyer for their hospitality during the photo shoot.

Diana Lischer-Goodband and Ezekiel Goodband were gracious shepherds during my absences from Scott Farm.

Thank you to Elisabeth Schuman, Laura Grace, Linda Grocholwalski, Elise Kaplan, Wendy Leeds, and Linda Warren for their insightful reading and editorial comments on the manuscript in progress.

My thanks also to Katharine Cobey, Kathryn Alexander, Melissa Lumley, and Rebecca Rothfusz for their contributions to the manuscript.

My ongoing gratitude and thanks to my son, Wells, a family of friends, and my literary agent Linda Roghaar, who continue to support and encourage my efforts in wool and words.

A Spinnery Bookshelf: Our Favorite References

Our pattern collection was selected for knitters of all skill levels who have a working knowledge of basic knitting techniques. For more technical information, inspiration, and insight into the culture and craft of knitting, the Spinnery staff recommend these, their favorite reference texts.

Bourgeois, Ann & Eugene. *Fair Isle Sweaters Simplified*. Bothell, WA: Martingale, 2000.

Budd, Ann. *The Knitter's Handy Book of Patterns*. Loveland, CO: Interweave Press, 2002.

Bush, Nancy. *Folk Knitting in Estonia*. Loveland, CO: Interweave Press, 1999.

Fassett, Kaffe. *Glorious Color*, New York: Clarkson N. Potter, 1988.

Gibson-Roberts, Priscilla. *Knitting in the Old Way*. Loveland, CO: Interweave Press, 1985.

Harrell, Betsy. *Anatolian Knitting Designs*. Istanbul: Redhouse Press, 1981.

LeCount, Cynthia. *Andean Folk Knitting*. St. Paul, MN: Dos Tejedoras, 1993.

Lind, Vibeke. *Knitting in the Nordic Tradition*. Asheville, NC: Lark Books, 1984.

Parry-Jones, Maria. *The Knitting Stitch Bible*. Iola, WI: Krause Publications, 2002.

Robinson, Debby. *The Encyclopedia of Knitting Techniques*. London: Swallow Publishing , 1987.

Rutt, Rev. Richard. *History of Handknitting*. Loveland, CO: Interweave Press, 1987.

Square, Vicki. *The Knitter's Companion*. Loveland, CO: Interweave Press, 1996.

Starmore, Alice. *Charts for Color Knitting*. Achmore, Isle of Lewis, Scotland: Windfall Press, 1992.

Takle, Tone, and Leslie Kolstad. *Sweaters: 28 Contemporary Designs in the Norwegian Tradition*. Loveland, CO: Interweave Press, 1992.

———. *More Sweaters: A Riot of Color, Pattern and Form*. Loveland, CO: Interweave Press, 1994.

Vogue Knitting: The Ultimate Knitting Book. New York: Sixth&Spring Books, 2002.

Walker, Barbara G. *A Treasury of Knitting Patterns, 1968*. Pittsville, WI: Schoolhouse Press, 1998.

———. *A Second Treasury of Knitting Patterns, 1970*. Pittsville, WI: Schoolhouse Press, 1998.

Zimmerman, Elizabeth. *The Knitter's Almanac*. New York: Dover Publications, 1974.

———. *Knitting Without Tears*. New York: Simon & Schuster, 1971.

DISCARD